Tea-Time Journeys

GAIL GRECO'S
LITTLE
Bed & Breakfast
COOKBOOK SERIES

Tea-Time Journeys

Text by GAIL GRECO

Photographs by TOM BAGLEY

RUTLEDGE HILL PRESS
Nashville, Tennessee

Copyright © 1997 by Gail Greco

Published in Nashville, Tennessee, by Rutledge Hill Press, Inc., 211 Seventh Avenue North, Nashville, Tennessee 37219. Distributed in Canada by H. B. Fenn & Company, Ltd., 34 Nixon Road, Bolton, Ontario L7E 1W2. Distributed in Australia by Millennium Books, 33 Maddox Street, Alexandria NSW 2015. Distributed in New Zealand by Tandem Press, 2 Rugby Road, Birkenhead, Auckland 10. Distributed in the United Kingdom by Verulam Publishing, Ltd., 152a Park Street Lane, Park Street, St. Albans, Hertfordshire AL2 2AU.

Editorial assistance by Tricia Conaty

Prop assistance by Camden Pottery of Camden, Maine

Photo on page xii by Lynn A. Herrmann and courtesy of Herb Haus B&B

Cover and book design by Gore Studio, Inc.

Text layout and typesetting by John Wilson Design

ON THE FRONT COVER: TEACUPS AND THE SHIP'S LOG ON BOARD THE *PAULINE* IN ROCKLAND, MAINE. RECIPE ON PAGE 16.

PICTURE FACING TITLE PAGE: RAVENWOOD CASTLE, NEW PLYMOUTH, OHIO

Library of Congress Cataloging-in-Publication Data

Greco, Gail.
    Tea-time journeys / text by Gail Greco; photographs by Tom Bagley.
        p. cm.
    Includes index.
    ISBN 1-55853-473-3 (hardcover)
    1. Afternoon teas. 2. Bed and breakfast accommodations—United States—Directories.   I. Title.
TX736.G744   1997
641.5'3—dc21
                                      97-583
                                      CIP

Printed in the United States of America

1 2 3 4 5 6 7 8 9 — 00 99 98 97

Other Books in This Series

∽◦∾

Vive la French Toast!
Autumn at the Farmers Market
Chocolates on the Pillow
Recipes for Romance
Gardens of Plenty

Contents

Shrimp, Tarragon, and Sweet
Corn Cake Sandwiches

Tuna, Potato, and Green Onion on Rye

Chicken, Capers, and Artichoke
Sandwiches

Grilled Mushroom and
Herb Tea Sandwiches

Fruit and Vegetable Sandwiches on
Raisin Bread

Pineapple, Sweet Red Pepper,
and Mint Sandwiches

Tea-Filled Meatballs with
Spicy Dipping Sauce

Medieval High Tea Beef Pie

UNCOMMON CONFECTIONS

Scottish Raspberry Buns

English Toffee Shortbread with
Chocolate Frosting

Lemon Shortbread Baked in a Pie Plate

Orange Saffron Pound Cake with
Orange Custard Sauce

Poppy Seed Pound Cake with
Orange Glaze

Whole-Wheat Pound Cake

Brownie Pound Cake

Java Chip Bundt Cake with Vanilla Icing

Chocolate Swirl Cake with
Chocolate Glaze

Rhubarb and Berry Sour Cream Nut Cake

Plum and Nectarine Crisp

Sweet Prune Cakes with Buttermilk
Vanilla Sauce

Spiced Tea Cake with Raspberry Filling
and Chocolate Frosting

Raspberry and Toasted Almond Bread
Pudding with Caramel Sauce

Peanut Butter Cheesecake with Chocolate
Glaze

TEA-TIME PANTRY

Sundried Tomato Pâté

Cucumber Basil Cheese Spread

Cheesy Crab Dip

Smoked Trout Dip

Plum Conserve

Beach Plum Jelly

Ginger Peach Chutney

Citrus Sorbet with Ginger Lime Sauce

Buttermint Cookies

Raspberry Muffins

DIRECTORY

INDEX

The Test Kitchen for the Cooking Association of Country Inns

Although inn recipes are tried-and-true and served at the inns all the time, the recipes in this cookbook have been further verified and tested for accuracy and clarification for the home kitchen.

The cooking seal of approval that accompanies this book means that every recipe has been tested in kitchens other than the source and that the association test kitchen has been satisfied that the recipe is proven and worthy of preparing.

The test kitchen is under the leadership of association founder Gail Greco. The prestigious list of kitchen testers is as follows:

∽◦∾

TRICIA CONATY, *Chef*
Cooking Association of Country Inns

DEB COZAN, *Chef*
Ravenwood Castle • New Plymouth, Ohio

SALLY KRUEGER, *Chef/Owner*
The Inn at 410 • Flagstaff, Arizona

A Tale to Tell about a Teacup

Teacups have a soul. The minute someone holds one by the handle and takes a first sip from its inviting rim, the teacup is ready to be of service; it has a purpose, and you can bet that somewhere the rites of friendship are about to be exchanged.

Tea-time makes memories. Many of mine come from the inns. I think of innkeeper Deedy Marble of the Governor's Inn in Ludlow, Vermont, who loved her teacup collection so much that she immortalized it on a spectacular note card. I think of the Gingerbread Mansion in Ferndale, California, and its afternoon tea table brimming with all different teacups and saucers—for any mood. And I can still feel the luxury of a butler tea service and splendid finger foods at Keswick Hall in Charlottesville, Virginia.

Taking time for tea—whether at an inn or in your own home—brews up passion, reflection, and conversation. In this, my second book on tea at inns, I have brought you a wider range of tea ideas with the underlying philosophy that enjoying tea-time is like taking a journey.

Tea is inspiring and encouraging, taking you away from the stress of daily life. I have tempted you here to take time and make a personal journey with a cup of tea. Indulge in sweets that stir creativity in the "Uncommon Confections" and the "Rise to the Occasion" chapters. Stepping over the traditional line to serve a casual high tea is another stress deflector. "Tea-Time Crossings" crosses over traditional tea-time sweets with unusual savory finger foods.

In "Saucer's Apprentice," I have brought helpful ideas for beverages that are acceptable to serve even during an elegant tea. The "Tea-Time Pantry" section is full of cookies and condiments that are meant to complement your tea should a friend stop by unexpectedly.

I have the inns to thank for their many terrific recipes. And as usual in this little bed-and-breakfast cookbook series, I wanted to add my own recipes as a means of giving back. In addition, I want to share something more with you. I believe we all have a tale to tell about a teacup, and here is my most personal story and the one to which I dedicate this book:

Teacups for Tuesdays
A Special Dedication

My mother's teacups are still in service. When she died, except for her artwork, what I wanted as keepsakes most of all were the individual cups and saucers with matching dessert plates that lined her precious old country hutch. To me, there wasn't anything else she owned that was more valuable, because the teacups reflected who she was. Each was simple yet elegant, unpretentious and genuine, with an inner and outward beauty—just like Mom's—that everyone agreed was rare.

Mom was very particular about her collection. There had to be a matching dessert plate with the cup and saucer; the set had to be in mint condition; and there had to be something curiously artistic about it. Mom only collected what she needed. Every time she bought a three-piece set, she showed it off as if it were a personal success—an achievement and a reaffirmation of her individuality. Her teacups seemed to hold her essence, and I wanted them—so as not to feel her loss so greatly. But as I discovered, the teacups had another assignment—a far greater one than sitting on the shelves of my cupboard.

You see, while Mom rejoiced in collecting the cups, her purpose was to use them. And from antique to new, use them she did in a very special way.

I always told my mother how fortunate she was to be part of a "sewing circle" as she and her friends called it: a group of women, who made the difficult effort of ensuring they got together once a week—despite juggling kids, dinners, and jobs. These days such weekly get-togethers are almost unheard of. Yet Mom's sewing circle members have kept it up for more than twenty-five years—even though they are the first to admit they never really sewed a thing.

Each member would go her own separate way except for a few hours every Tuesday night when their worlds came together in great harmony and no one could separate them. Through the years, there were some changes in the group. But there was a nucleus of eight who held fast and

loyal and helped each other through life's ups and downs. They developed an acceptance of and love for one another. "The girls," as the husbands called them, watched their children grow up and their children's children; and they watched each other grow up—but they always stayed together.

Joan C., Florence, Jo, Arlene, Joan P., Jean, Dolores, and Kathy—the girls Mom's teacups served—took turns hosting the get-together at their homes on Tuesday nights. And for many of those years, my mother's teacups served them well each time the meeting was at Mom's home. Each tea set had its own simple beauty. I was particularly fond of one Mom had purchased at a garage sale: a bone china with a cheerful country, hand-painted design. She giggled with delight the day she made her little find. It cost her pennies. It made her feel like a million when she served with it.

In the weeks before my mother's death, the girls held onto their Tuesday night ritual—even though Mom was too weak to go to any of their houses. They brought the evening to my mother's bedside in picnic baskets full of things to eat. Mom could hardly stay awake during those last few Tuesdays, but she managed a smile—she was together with her girls.

The group refused to believe they were losing her and found a creative way to hold on for just a little longer. Keeping the Tuesday night ritual was their way of fighting back and saying, "No, this is not happening." But it was, and during this awful time, each needed a part of my mother, too.

So, when my mother left us, I looked at the teacups and knew they could no longer be of service as they had been before. And while I wanted them all, an idea took hold of me. The teacups my mother's friends had sipped from over the years were symbolic, and each of the girls would have to have one like a parting gift from a beloved friend. It would ease their pain. I knew my sister also wanted the teacups, but she embraced the idea fully. We would give them up—and yet there were enough for the both of us to have three sets each of our very own. We divided the others up, according to personalities. For example, a gilded white, dainty old-world cup went to Joan C. for her European flair and travel; a bold, striped-and-floral contemporary teacup went to Florence for her avant garde ideas and creativity; the odd-shaped teacup with the thatched roof cottage design went to Kathy for her enjoyment of quaint things and bed-and-breakfast inns; and a floral design by Lenox went to Jo for her impeccable taste in everything. We knew the girls well—for we all socialized as families beyond the Tuesday night get-togethers.

My sister and I schemed as to how to present the girls with their gifts from Mom. We decided to treat them to a picnic in their honor at Mom's house for a final Tuesday evening. We bought decorative Victorian hatboxes and filled them with straw. A tea set sat on top of the straw, surrounded by a picture of Mom, a pot full of her favorite African violets, and a blank journal—the latter for them to record their Tuesday night remembrances.

The teacups in the hatboxes were lined up on the hutch, not far from where Mom had always displayed them, only now, they would be carried away to find new homes. No one deserved Mom's teacups more, and my sister and I felt we had served Mom well. The girls, well, you can only imagine how they felt, receiving them on a Tuesday night—even though one member of the group was painfully absent.

I brought my own three teacups, saucers, and dessert plates back to my home. At first, I displayed them on my sideboard in a look-but-don't-touch position. Then I realized there was a grand design in my inheriting only three. To make an even number for my own entertaining, I would need another set. Well, I think Mom was looking down and figured if I could hunt down my own teacups, I could experience what she did—the peace and comfort in finding a part of yourself in a teacup. I realized I could begin to make the collection mine and keep the enchantment of her life ever bright and shining.

So, I have started the search for at least a fourth set. It isn't easy finding three matching pieces, but it wasn't easy for Mom either. I'm hoping to come home one day from a garage sale or antiques store and laugh as she did with delight at my find. Good things—like the friendships that the sewing circle formed or the bonds that may be found in your own tea-time journeys—truly don't come easily.

Saucer's Apprentice

Apple Berry Tea

ᢁᢍᢩ

Hot or cold, this blend of tea and fruit juice is perfectly harmonized, and that's just the way guests feel after taking a few sips.

8	quality raspberry (or blackberry) tea bags		2	teaspoons pure honey
2	cups just-boiled water		4	cups pure apple juice

MAKES 6 TO 8 SERVINGS

Place the tea bags in a teapot. Pour in the boiling water and steep for 5 minutes. Squeeze excess tea from tea bags and discard. Stir in the honey and the apple juice. Heat to serving temperature, but do not boil. Serve in individual teacups.

—THE KING'S COTTAGE

IT'S TIME FOR APPLE BERRY TEA AND SWEETS IN A KING'S COTTAGE GUEST ROOM.

PICTURE FACING CHAPTER OPENER: TEA IN THE GARDEN AT THE HERB HAUS IN FREDERICKSBURG, TEXAS

Orange Clove Tea

～∞～

Pitchers full of this delicious tea make their way regularly onto the wooden front porch of the inn. Sips are taken between "rockings" in a wicker chair.

3 to 4	teaspoons loose orange pekoe or black tea		1	orange, sliced into ¹/₂-inch-thick pieces, each piece cut in half
1	quart just-boiled water			Whole cloves

MAKES 6 SERVINGS

Steep the tea in the just-boiled water for about five minutes. Stud the orange slice rinds generously with whole cloves and place the slices in 6 teacups. Strain the hot tea directly into the prepared cups. Serve immediately.

—THE INN AT MAPLEWOOD FARM

For an interesting tea-time drink, brew tea in apple cider. Place a quality cinnamon or spiced tea bag into a saucepan with 1 cup of cider. Heat over medium-high heat for about five minutes. Simmer 3 to 5 minutes more. Add a little extra cinnamon and cloves if desired. Serve in a mug; discard the bag.

Spiced Rum Tea

✈

The flavor of this tea is best described as something like a hot toddy.

6	teaspoons loose orange pekoe or black tea	1½	pints just-boiled water
½	teaspoon ground cloves	3	teaspoons quality dark rum

MAKES 6 SERVINGS

Place the tea and the cloves in a small saucepan. Add 1 cup of the just-boiled water and steep for 5 minutes. Pour a little tea into 6 teacups, and then fill the cups with the remaining boiling water. Add a splash of rum to each cup and serve.

—THE INN AT MAPLEWOOD FARM

Herbal Bouquet Tea

✈

Here, an assortment of herbs that have been dried make an interesting cup of tea.

2	cups dried lemon verbena leaves	3	tablespoons whole cloves, crushed
1	cup dried chamomile	1	(6-inch) cinnamon stick, crushed
1	cup dried orange peel	1	quart water

MAKES 1 QUART DRIED TEA

Combine all of the ingredients, except the water, in a large bowl. Mix well. Store the tea in a tightly covered tin. When you are ready to prepare a cup of tea, shake the tin well. Spoon 1 teaspoon of the tea mixture for each cup of water into a teapot. Pour boiling water over the tea. Steep for 5 to 10 minutes. Strain and serve.

—HERB HAUS BED & BREAKFAST

Chai

Chai is the perfect, lighter version of a café latte. At coffee bars, chai has replaced espresso, the Pacific Northwest's trendiest beverage.

1	quart whole milk
1	teaspoon cinnamon
1/2	teaspoon cardamom
1	teaspoon ground almonds
1/3	cup honey
1	quart water
8	teaspoons loose orange pekoe or black tea

MAKES 6 TO 8 SERVINGS

In a large saucepan, combine the milk, cinnamon, cardamom, and almonds. Simmer for 1/2 hour, stirring occasionally. Add the honey and then immediately remove the brew from the heat. In a separate saucepan, boil 1 quart of water. Pour the boiling water into a teapot with the pekoe or black tea. Steep for 5 minutes. Add the hot milk mixture to the tea in a ratio of 1 to 1. Pour back and forth between the 2 containers to mix. Return the mixture to the teapot and strain before serving.

—THE INN AT MAPLEWOOD FARM

Sherry Tea

Sometimes I cannot make up my mind whether I want a spot of sherry with a twist of lemon in the late afternoon or a simple cup of orange pekoe. This recipe solved my dilemma.

1	heaping tablespoon orange pekoe tea	1	pint cold water
1	quart boiling water	1	cinnamon stick
6	large lemons	1	cup sugar
		2 to 3	cups cream sherry

MAKES 10 TO 12 SERVINGS

Steep the tea in boiling water for 15 minutes. Meanwhile, extract the juice from the lemons, reserving the shells. In a medium saucepan, combine the lemon juice, lemon shells, cold water, and the cinnamon stick. Simmer until the lemon shells are tender. Strain and return the mixture to the saucepan. Add the sugar, stirring until it dissolves. Strain the tea and add it to the lemon mixture. Add the sherry just before serving. Serve hot.

—GAIL'S KITCHEN

May Wine with Sweet Woodruff and Violas

ᓚᢛᘏᣔ

The first time I had this libation, I sat with a dear friend. We "philosophized" about changes in our lives and a bright future full of simple pleasures. May wine is of Germanic origin and was originally made by ancient folks with sweet woodruff, which they said made one merry. Indeed, the single glass Trish and I enjoyed one spring gave us much pause for promises. This recipe will serve a tea party, but you can also make it by the individual glass. I have included strawberries and violas in the recipe, because that is the way it was first served to me.

12	sprigs sweet woodruff	1	quart dessert or other light champagne or carbonated water
3	pints small strawberries (cut large ones in half)		
1¼	cups powdered sugar	1	pint or more edible violas or Johnny-jump-ups
3	750-milliliter bottles Rhine wine		

MAKES 1 PUNCH BOWL FULL

Place the sweet woodruff and strawberries in the bottom of a large bowl along with the powdered sugar and 1 of the bottles of Rhine wine. Stir the mixture and cover. Refrigerate for no more than 30 minutes. Place a block of ice or a few trays of ice cubes into a punch bowl. Pour the mixture over the ice and add the remaining wine and champagne. Float violas on top and serve in punch glasses or non-fluted champagne glasses. Add a strawberry and viola to each glass.

—GAIL'S KITCHEN

Tea-Time's Flaming Brandy Café

~∞~

Tea-time is not for everyone. So when you have a few in the crowd who would prefer coffee, serve them something other than an ordinary cup of coffee.

1	lemon	3	sugar cubes
1	(3-inch) cinnamon stick	4$^1/_2$	ounces brandy
8	whole cloves	3	cups freshly brewed, hot coffee

MAKES 8 CUPS

With a sharp knife, carefully remove the lemon rind in one long spiral. Place the spiral rind in a chafing dish with the cinnamon stick, cloves, and sugar cubes. Cook over direct heat. In a heated ladle, ignite the brandy and pour it over the lemon-sugar mixture. Continue ladling flaming brandy until the sugar is dissolved. Gradually add the coffee, and continue ladling the brandy until the flame fades. Serve immediately.

—GAIL'S KITCHEN

If you have never been to a tea tasting, you must get to John Harney & Sons, a private-label master tea blender, who supplies many inns and some of the world's grandest hotels. It's something like a winery; you get to sample various teas at the tea showroom, 11 East Main Street; Salisbury, Connecticut. Call 1-800-Tea-Time. Oh, and ask for their book about reading tea leaves. It is fascinating!

Spirited Apple Cider

✺

Here is a festive addition to a tea party that has lots of "punch" appeal.

12	whole cloves	1	cup freshly squeezed orange juice	
6	whole allspice berries	1	cup cranberry juice cocktail	
3	(2½-inch) cinnamon sticks, broken	1	cup pineapple juice	
1	tablespoon grated orange peel	½	cup dark rum	
8	cups fresh apple cider	½	cup apple-flavored brandy	

MAKES 8 CUPS

Make a cheesecloth bundle of cloves, allspice, cinnamon sticks, and orange peel. Place in a Dutch oven and add the apple cider. Bring to a boil over high heat. Reduce the heat to medium, and cook for 15 minutes, or until the liquid is reduced to 4 cups. Remove and discard the spice bundle. Stir in the orange juice and the remaining ingredients. Simmer until thoroughly heated. Serve warm.

—GAIL'S KITCHEN

Tea, which is some 5,000 years old, is poured into glasses or cups to the tune of 180 cups for every American per year, according to the Tea Council of the U.S.A.

Apple Sangria

꼭

Herb Haus prepares this recipe with their own Fredericksburg, Texas, Native Herb Tea, but our testers substituted with a few different fruit-based herbal teas and enjoyed the recipe. If you want to order the B&B's special tea, see the directory for information.

2	medium oranges
2	medium lemons
1/3	cup sugar
1	(6-ounce) can frozen apple juice concentrate, thawed

3	cups prepared Fredericksburg, Texas, Native Herb Tea, cooled
2	cups sparkling water

MAKES 8 SERVINGS

Juice 1 of the oranges and 1 of the lemons. Combine the juices and set aside. Cut the remaining orange and lemon into thin slices and place them in a large pitcher. Sprinkle the slices with sugar and crush them with a wooden spoon. Stir in the reserved fruit juices, apple juice concentrate, and prepared tea. Stir in sparkling water to taste. To serve, pour the Sangria into individual, ice-filled glasses.

—HERB HAUS BED & BREAKFAST

Freeze edible flowers in ice trays and serve with iced tea. This makes for a pleasant surprise for the tea drinker.

Rising
to the
Occasion

∽◦∾

Gingered Cranberry and Poppy Seed Spice Bread

✎

Crystallized ginger is kept on board the *Pauline* just in case anyone gets a little queasy. Ginger will not calm waters, but it will calm the tummy. Chef Emily Franklin has the enviable job of working on the ship, and I marveled at how she orchestrates even entire meals from a kitchen smaller than a clothes closet. With all that ginger, it's no wonder she created this recipe. Our testers suggest doubling the butter for a more moist bread, if you don't mind the added calories.

1¼	cups all-purpose flour		2	tablespoons butter, softened
1	teaspoon salt		1½	cups dried cranberries
1	teaspoon baking soda		1	cup sugar
1	teaspoon cinnamon		¼	cup sliced, crystallized ginger
1	egg		2	tablespoons poppy seeds
1	cup milk			

MAKES 1 LOAF

*I*n a large mixing bowl, combine the flour, salt, baking soda, and cinnamon. Add the egg, milk, and butter, mixing well. In a separate bowl, combine the cranberries, sugar, and ginger. Add to the flour mixture, stirring well. Turn the batter into a greased 9x5-inch loaf pan and sprinkle the top with poppy seeds. Bake at 375° for 40 minutes or until the cake is browned on the top.

—THE *PAULINE*

PICTURE FACING CHAPTER OPENER: CRANBERRY BUTTERMILK SCONES RISE TO THE OCCASION AT THE INN AT MAPLEWOOD FARM. RECIPE ON PAGE 26.
LEFT: TAKING TEA ON THE UPPER DECK

Apricot Almond Bread

⋘⋙

Sometimes things get tipsy on the *Pauline* as a wave or two passes by and the teacups shake just a wee bit. That's when it's nice to have a steady bread you can count on like this one. Even at home, when things get rocky, make up this bread and you will find calm waters. Serve with a spread of apple butter for added interest.

2	cups dried apricots, cut into thin slices	1	teaspoon salt
1½	cups just-boiled water	2½	cups all-purpose flour
¼	cup (½ stick) butter	1	teaspoon baking soda
1	cup sugar	1	egg
		1	cup slivered almonds

MAKES 1 LOAF

Preheat the oven to 350°. Coat a 9x5-inch loaf pan (or 2 small loaf pans) with cooking oil spray. Set aside.

Place the apricots in a large bowl and pour in the just-boiled water. Add the butter, sugar, and salt. Stir well. Allow the mixture to cool slightly, then add the flour, baking soda, and egg. Mix by hand until the batter is smooth. Pour the batter into the prepared loaf pan. Sprinkle slivered almonds over the top. Bake for 1 hour, or until the almonds are a golden brown and a tester comes clean.

—THE *PAULINE*

TEACUPS AND THE SHIP'S LOG

Honey Banana Raisin Bread

✀

Tea and banana bread go together, and the banana provides such a natural sweetener that little sugar is needed. But I particularly like this recipe, because it pairs the wholesomeness of the banana with honey and raisins. I agree with innkeeper Mike Tyler's assessment that this bread is not overly moist like most banana bread recipes. Five chefs' hats to the Wild Swan Inn for this twist on a traditional favorite.

2¼	cups all-purpose flour		½	cup margarine
1	tablespoon baking powder		1	egg
½	teaspoon cinnamon		1	teaspoon vanilla extract
½	teaspoon ground nutmeg		¾	cup raisins
½	teaspoon salt		½	cup coarsely chopped walnuts
⅓	cup pure honey		3	ripe bananas, mashed

MAKES 1 LOAF

*P*reheat the oven to 350°. In a large mixing bowl, combine the flour, baking powder, cinnamon, nutmeg, and salt. In a separate bowl, whip the honey and margarine until thoroughly blended. Add the egg and the vanilla, stirring well. Gently fold the raisins and walnuts into the flour mixture. Add ⅓ of the bananas and ⅓ of the honey-egg mixture. Stir gently until combined. Repeat, alternating banana and honey-egg mixture until the ingredients are well-blended. Do not overmix.

Coat a 9x5-inch loaf pan with cooking oil spray. Pour the batter into the pan. Bake for 50 to 55 minutes, or until golden brown and a tester comes clean. Cool on a wire rack.

—WILD SWAN INN

Glazed Lemon Herbal Tea Bread

༄

Company finds the bread refreshing and paired well with an herbal tea or fresh iced tea.

Bread

3/4	cup milk
1	tablespoon chopped fresh lemon verbena
1	tablespoon chopped fresh lemon thyme (or 1 teaspoon dried thyme)
1/2	cup butter
3/4	cup sugar
2	eggs

2	cups all-purpose flour
1 1/2	teaspoons baking powder
1/4	teaspoon salt
1	tablespoon grated lemon peel

Glaze

1	cup sifted powdered sugar
2	tablespoons fresh lemon juice

Assembly

Fresh mint for garnish

MAKES 1 LOAF

Combine the milk, lemon verbena, and thyme in a medium saucepan; bring to a boil. Remove from the heat and cover. Allow the mixture to stand for about 5 minutes, then cool completely. In bowl of electric mixer, cream the butter, adding the sugar gradually. When the butter and sugar are well blended, add the eggs, one at a time, beating well after each addition.

Preheat the oven to 325°. In a mixing bowl, combine the flour, baking powder, and salt. Add the dry ingredients to the butter mixture alternately with the milk mixture, making sure to begin and end with the flour mixture. Stir well after each addition. When the ingredients are fully combined, stir in the lemon peel.

Turn the batter into a greased and floured 9x5-inch loaf pan. Bake for 50 minutes, or until golden and a tester comes clean. Cool the cake on a wire rack for about 10 minutes, then remove the bread from the pan and cool completely.

Meanwhile, prepare the glaze. Combine the powdered sugar and lemon juice in a mixing bowl. Stir until smooth. Drizzle the glaze over the cooled bread. Serve by the slice, garnished with fresh mint.

—GAIL'S KITCHEN

Raspberry Lemon Oat Muffins

∽o∾

The oats give this muffin an unforgettably good texture; and since I am a fan of lemon and raspberry, this recipe has become a favorite. The muffins freeze well. Part of the batter needs a one-hour resting time before baking.

2	cups quick oats
2	cups buttermilk
1	cup packed light brown sugar
3/4	cup butter, melted and cooled
3	eggs, slightly beaten
1 1/2	cups all-purpose flour
2	teaspoons baking powder
1/2	teaspoon salt
3/4	teaspoon baking soda
1 1/2	cups fresh raspberries
1	teaspoon grated lemon peel

MAKES 24 MUFFINS

In a large mixing bowl, combine the oats and the buttermilk. Sprinkle the brown sugar over the top and set the mixture aside for 1 hour. Preheat the oven to 400°. Mix together the melted butter and the eggs until well blended. Add to the oats-buttermilk mixture, stirring well. In a separate bowl, combine the flour, baking powder, salt, and baking soda. Gradually stir the dry ingredients into the oat mixture. When the batter is thoroughly combined, gently fold in the raspberries and the lemon peel. Coat muffin tins with cooking oil spray. Fill muffin tins 2/3 full with batter. Bake for 20 to 25 minutes, or until tester comes clean.

—THE QUEEN ANNE INN

Never cut a scone open with a knife. Instead, break it in half by hand. Then slather each piece with preserves and cream, only when you're ready to take a bite.

Mini-Butterscotch Muffins

⌣o⌣

Like a favorite old blanket or quilt, butterscotch desserts bring back warm, comforting thoughts—perfect with a warm, steaming cup of fresh tea. This recipe makes many muffins, but they are small and they freeze well. Do not use the larger butterscotch chips, they are too big for the muffins. But if you make these in regular muffin tins, you can use the larger chips.

1	cup quick oats
2	cups buttermilk
1¼	cups light brown sugar
¾	cup butter, melted and cooled
3	eggs, slightly beaten
1½	cups all-purpose flour
2	teaspoons baking powder
1	scant teaspoon baking soda
½	teaspoon salt
¾	cup mini-butterscotch chips

MAKES 6 DOZEN

*M*ix together the oats and buttermilk in a large bowl. Add the brown sugar to the bowl by sprinkling it on top; allow the mixture to stand for 1 hour.

Preheat the oven to 400°. In a large bowl, just whisk to mix the butter with the eggs and set aside. In a separate bowl, sift together the flour, baking powder, baking soda, and salt. Set aside. Combine the egg and oat mixtures. Add the flour mixture, stirring gently. Fold in the butterscotch chips. Spoon the batter into several lightly greased mini-muffin tins. Bake 7 to 10 minutes, or until golden.

—THE QUEEN ANNE INN

*T*ea is becoming a major cooking ingredient incorporated into everything from cakes and breads to rice dishes and meat sauces, according to the Tea Council of America. Get yourself a copy of Cooking with Tea at bookstores. It is a cookbook incorporating all kinds of herbal teas into traditional dishes. The book is by Celestial Seasonings Teas; so most of the recipes call for using their brand of tea.

Sweet Molasses Muffins

꩜

Hearty muffins are a welcome sweet on board the *Pauline*. The chef serves them during tea-time and sometimes with breakfast. I was attracted to this recipe because the molasses offers the muffins a deep, smoky taste that complements nearly any flavor of tea.

2	egg whites
1/4	cup molasses
2	tablespoons canola oil
1	cup milk
2	cups all-purpose flour

1/4	cup brown sugar, plus extra for topping
1	teaspoon salt
2	teaspoons baking soda

MAKES 10 TO 12 MUFFINS

*P*reheat the oven to 350°. Mix together the egg whites, molasses, oil, and milk. In a separate bowl, combine the flour, brown sugar, salt, and baking soda. Add the dry ingredients to the molasses mixture, stirring until smooth. Spoon the batter into greased standard muffin tins. Press about a teaspoon of brown sugar onto the top of each muffin. Bake for 15 minutes, or until tester comes clean.

—THE *PAULINE*

LEFT: MUFFINS AND A MARITIME VIEW OF THE ROCKLAND, MAINE HARBOR FROM THE PILOT'S PERCH ON THE PAULINE

Cranberry Buttermilk Scones

◦⌣◦

Try these cranberry scones with the spiced rum tea (page 4) on a cold afternoon. Memories of this inn come to mind when I make these scones. I see myself driving up to the classic farmhouse with the warmest of innkeepers greeting me. I know I'm in for a peaceful repast.

CHAI AND SCONES IN THE DINING ROOM OF THE INN AT
MAPLEWOOD FARM IN HILLSBOROUGH, NEW HAMPSHIRE

2	cups all-purpose flour
1/3	cup sugar
1 1/2	teaspoons baking powder
1/2	teaspoon baking soda
1/4	teaspoon salt
6	separated tablespoons unsalted butter, chilled
1/2	cup buttermilk
1	egg
1 1/2	teaspoons vanilla extract
2/3	cup dried cranberries

MAKES 8 SCONES

Preheat the oven to 400°. In a large mixing bowl, combine the flour, sugar, baking powder, baking soda, and salt. Cut the butter into 1/2-inch cubes and distribute over the flour mixture. With a pastry blender, cut in the butter until coarse crumbs form.

In a small bowl, stir together the buttermilk, egg, and vanilla. Add the buttermilk mixture to the flour mixture, stirring well to combine. Stir in the dried fruit.

With lightly floured hands, pat the dough into a 1-inch-thick circle and arrange on an ungreased baking sheet. Cut into 8 wedges. Bake for 20 minutes, or until the top is slightly browned. Cool on a wire rack.

—THE INN AT MAPLEWOOD FARM

To make a strong tea latte, you can pair 4 cups boiling water with 7 tablespoons of black Thai tea leaves and 4 teaspoons of condensed milk. Steep the tea leaves in the water and strain through a filter. Stir 1 teaspoon of the milk into 4 glasses. Add the tea. Serve immediately. This recipe is from the Inn at Maplewood Farm.

Yogurt and Sunflower Scones with Fruit and Nuts

❦

It's hard to think of a scone not having fat in it. Scones are meant for indulging and for slathering on the cream as a seasoned bricklayer does his mortar. So why a yogurt scone? The Inn at 410, known for its quality cooking and creative dishes, has even won culinary awards and has devised a way to lower the fat content and offer a no-guilt scone.

YOGURT AND SUNFLOWER SCONES WITH FRUIT AND NUTS FROM THE INN AT 410 IN FLAGSTAFF, ARIZONA.

1½	cups all-purpose flour	½	cup toasted sunflower seeds
½	teaspoon baking powder	½	cup white chocolate chips
½	teaspoon baking soda	1	egg, slightly beaten
⅛	teaspoon salt	½	cup plain nonfat yogurt
3	tablespoons margarine, chilled and cut into small pieces	½	teaspoon fresh lemon peel
¾	cup finely chopped mixed-dried tropical fruit	6	teaspoons sugar
¼	cup finely chopped dried pineapple		

MAKES 12 SCONES

Preheat the oven to 400°. Coat a baking sheet with cooking oil spray.

In a large bowl, combine the flour, baking powder, baking soda, and salt. Using a pastry blender or 2 knives, cut in the margarine until coarse crumbs form. Stir in the mixed fruit, dried pineapple, sunflower seeds, and chocolate chips. Set aside

In a medium bowl, whisk together the egg, yogurt, lemon peel, and sugar. Add to the flour mixture and whisk just until moistened. Wetting hands, shape the dough into a round ball. Divide the dough in half and roll out each half to ½-inch thickness. Using a 2-inch biscuit cutter, cut out scones and place slightly apart on the baking sheet. Bake 15 to 20 minutes, or until scones are golden brown and tester comes clean. Cool on a wire rack.

—THE INN AT 410

"Tea isn't result-oriented; it is a process; no agenda, goals, or expectations. . . . You are no longer in conflict; therefore you become more subtle and graceful in the ways you express yourself. . . . This is an extremely sensuous feeling," says Alexandra Stoddard in her book, Tea Celebrations. *I love this little book about life, tea, and simple pleasures.*

Sugarplum Scones

Don't let the name fool you. These Christmastime biscuits are festive any time of year. Prunes, vanilla, and cream make up a scone that is also delicious during the summer months, when I have served it with spiced iced tea.

2	cups all-purpose flour	1	egg
1/4	cup sugar	1 1/2	teaspoons vanilla extract
2	teaspoons baking powder	3/4	cup chopped, pitted prunes
1/8	teaspoon salt	1/2	cup powdered sugar
1/3	cup unsalted butter, chilled		
1/2	cup heavy cream		

MAKES 14 SCONES

Preheat the oven to 425°. In a large mixing bowl, combine the flour, sugar, baking powder, and salt. Cut the butter into 1/2-inch cubes and distribute over the flour mixture. With a pastry blender, cut in the butter until coarse crumbs form.

In a separate bowl, stir together the cream, egg, and vanilla. Add the cream mixture to the flour mixture and stir until combined. Fold in the prunes.

Transfer the dough to a lightly floured board and pat the dough into a 1/2-inch-thick circle. Using a star-shaped cookie cutter, press out the scones until all of the dough is used up. Place the scones on a lightly-greased baking sheet just slightly apart from one another. Bake for 13 to 15 minutes, or until lightly browned. While still warm, sprinkle the scones with powdered sugar until completely coated and white. Cool on a wire rack for 5 minutes. Serve warm.

—THE INN AT MAPLEWOOD FARM

LEFT:. . . WHILE SUGARPLUMS DANCED IN THEIR HEADS. . . .

*R*ose Petal Drop Scones with Beach Plum Jelly Icing

∽∾∽

Beach plum is a seacoast shrub with edible white flowers that blossom and produce plum-like fruit. Beach plums flourish in innkeeper Donna Stone's Cape Cod environment. In fact, Donna graces many breakfast recipes with beach plums, including a jelly which she incorporates into the icing for these cookie-sized scones. The jelly recipe is on page 100.

Scones

2¹/₄	cups unbleached all-purpose flour
2	teaspoons sugar
2	teaspoons baking powder
¹/₂	teaspoon baking soda
³/₄	teaspoon salt
¹/₂	teaspoon cinnamon
¹/₄	cup (¹/₂ stick) unsalted butter
¹/₃	cup coarsely ground pistachios (shelled and unsalted)

1	cup heavy cream
1	tablespoon rose water
2	tablespoons cleaned and finely shredded rose petals

Icing

1	cup powdered sugar
3	teaspoons rose water
1	tablespoon beach plum jelly (or substitute 1 tablespoon red currant jelly)

MAKES 24 COOKIE SCONES

*P*reheat the oven to 425°. In a large bowl, combine the flour, sugar, baking powder, baking soda, salt, and cinnamon. Cut in the butter and mix until coarse crumbs form. Stir in the pistachios.

In a separate bowl, combine the cream and the rose water. Stir in the shredded rose petals. Add the rose mixture to the dry ingredients. Stir until a soft dough forms. Drop dough by the teaspoonful onto an ungreased baking sheet. Bake 10 to 12 minutes, or until golden brown.

Prepare the icing. In a small bowl, combine the powdered sugar, rose water, and the beach

plum jelly. Whisk until smooth. Add another teaspoon of rose water if the mixture is too thick. Drizzle over the warm scones and serve.

—THE WILDFLOWER INN

THE BEACH ROSE ROOM IS SET FOR TEA AND ROMANCE AT THE WILDFLOWER INN ON CAPE COD.

Apple Cinnamon Scones

∽०∾

Rarely do you find a scone recipe that takes full advantage of apples. Moistened with apple juice as well as the fruit itself, this one bursts with apple flavor. Our testers found that the whole-wheat and oats give the scone a little more interest and texture. We also suggest adding a little more cinnamon, according to your taste, and more flour if dough is too thin.

$^1/_2$	cup all-purpose flour		1	green apple, peeled, cored, and minced
$^1/_2$	cup whole-wheat flour		1	cup old-fashioned rolled oats
$1^1/_2$	teaspoons baking powder		2	tablespoons apple juice
$1^1/_2$	teaspoons cinnamon		2	tablespoons honey
$^1/_3$	cup ($^3/_4$ stick) butter		2	teaspoons sugar
2	eggs			Egg wash

MAKES 12 SCONES

Preheat the oven to 350°. Combine all of the ingredients except the egg wash. Mix well until a dough forms. Transfer the dough to a 12-inch round greased pizza pan, patting out the dough to fit the pan. Brush the surface with egg wash and score the dough into 12 equal wedges. Bake for 20 to 25 minutes, or until golden. Let scones cool down and then cut through the scored wedges.

—ASA RANSOM HOUSE

Basil and Asiago Cheese Scones

୧୬ଡ଼ଠ

Tea is served with some ceremony at Asa Ransom, where afternoon tea is a part of the pampering. This scone makes delicious use of the Italian semisoft cheese known as Asiago. I found that the cheese imparts a nutty taste to the scone, perfectly complemented by the basil. In and of themselves, these scones make a nice savory for the tea-time table, or serve them with a tomato chutney.

1/4	cup shortening
2	teaspoons baking powder
2	cups all-purpose flour
2/3	cup buttermilk
1/2	cup grated Asiago cheese
1	tablespoon finely chopped fresh basil

MAKES 16 SCONES

Preheat the oven to 350°. In a large mixing bowl, cut together the shortening, baking powder, and flour. Add the buttermilk, cheese, and basil, mixing gently until a soft dough forms (do not overmix). Transfer the dough to a floured surface and pat into an 8-inch square. Cut the dough into 16 2-inch squares and place them on a greased baking sheet. Bake for about 30 minutes, or until golden.

—ASA RANSOM HOUSE

[*35*]

ROYAL PAMPERING AWAITS THOSE WHO CROSS THE DRAWBRIDGE AND ENTER RAVENWOOD CASTLE.

*T*eacups are terrific collectibles and give you a reason to stop at an antique shop on your travels. Look for teacups that have a matching lunch/dessert-size plate. Display the plate on a dish stand and place the teacup and saucer in front.

Savory Cheddar Cheese Scones

༽ᨆᨆᨆ

Nice alone or with butter or one of the many savory spreads in this book, these scones are also tasty with the ginger peach chutney on page 101.

2	cups all-purpose flour		1	cup shredded sharp Cheddar cheese
1	tablespoon baking powder		1	egg
1/2	teaspoon onion salt		1/2	cup light cream, plus extra for brushing
1	tablespoon dried parsley			
1/4	cup butter			

MAKES 8 TO 10 SCONES

Preheat the oven to 425°. In a large mixing bowl, combine the flour, baking powder, salt, and parsley. Cut in the butter until coarse crumbs form. Stir in the cheese, mixing until well combined. Add the egg and cream, stirring until a dough begins to form.

Transfer the dough to a lightly floured surface, and knead for about 1 minute. With a floured rolling pin, roll the dough out to 1/2 inch thick. Cut out the scones with a 2-inch biscuit cutter, until all the dough is used. Place the scones on a baking tray and brush the tops with a light coating of cream. Bake for 12 minutes, or until golden brown.

—RAVENWOOD CASTLE

Tea-Time Crossings

*H*erbed Cheese in Braided Bread Ring

ༀ

The scent of barley and hops baking permeates the air when you bake this bread. Then, remembrances of the Fearrington House brighten the whole tea-time experience. You will need to start preparing the bread a day ahead of serving time.

PICTURE FACING CHAPTER OPENER: ICED TEA WITH ROSEMARY AND CHÈVRE TEA SANDWICHES. RECIPE ON PAGE 48.

Herbed Cheese

12	ounces small-curd cottage cheese, drained
8	ounces cream cheese, softened
2	tablespoons sour cream
1	tablespoon heavy cream
1/4	cup mixed minced fresh herbs (basil, tarragon, chives, thyme, parsley)
2	cloves garlic, minced
2	scallions, minced
1/4	teaspoon salt
1/4	teaspoon freshly cracked white pepper

Bread Ring

1	12-ounce can beer of choice
1	rounded tablespoon yeast
1	cup or so warm water
6 to 8	cups unbleached flour
1	tablespoon salt
1	egg yolk, at room temperature

MAKES 10 TO 12 SERVINGS

*P*repare the herbed cheese. Work the cottage cheese in the bowl of a food processor until smooth. Add the cream cheese, sour cream, and heavy cream. Continue to process until the mixture is smooth. Blend the herbs, garlic, scallions, salt, and pepper with the cheese. Do not overwork or the cheese will become thin. Spread the mixture in a large, shallow, flat pan and cover. Refrigerate for 24 hours to allow the flavors to meld.

Prepare the bread. Warm the beer by running hot water over the can. In a large mixing bowl, combine the beer, yeast, and water. Allow the mixture to sit for a few minutes till the yeast bubbles. Add 4 cups of the flour or enough to form a thick paste (stir until a thick paste forms). Cover and set aside for 8 hours, or until the mixture rises and then falls down.

Add the remaining flour and salt. Let dough rise in a warm place for at least 1 hour. Mix thoroughly and turn the dough out onto a floured surface. Use a pastry scraper to keep turning the mixture until it becomes possible to knead. Pat the dough into a circle, fold in half, and knead for 12 to 13 minutes. Cut off 3 pieces of dough and roll them into long ropes about 1½ inches in diameter. Grease an 8-inch round cake pan and invert it onto a greased baking sheet. Braid 2 ropes of bread together around the outside of the cake pan. Use the third rope to make a bow. Cover and let rise for about 1 hour.

Preheat the oven to 375°. Brush with a paste made from the egg yolk and 2 teaspoons of water. Be careful not to let excess egg glaze collect between the bread and the cake pan, or it may keep the bread from rising properly. Bake for 35 minutes, or until golden brown. Allow the bread to cool.

To assemble the bread ring, mound the herbed cheese into the center of the freshly baked braided bread ring and serve with crackers or a knife to cut into the bread.

—THE FEARRINGTON HOUSE

*W*ild Mushroom Roll-Ups

⤞⊶⤝

Slices of moist bread serve as the dough for these clever savory rolls. I like the wilder side of mushrooms with crimini and chanterelles, but the recipe allows for your own personal choice. These are easy to eat, and be forewarned, they go very fast. The roll-ups need to chill in the refrigerator for three hours in advance of serving.

1	tablespoon butter			Salt and freshly cracked black pepper
1	½-inch slice Vidalia onion, finely chopped		1	loaf sliced white bread, crusts removed
1	cup finely chopped assorted wild mushrooms		½ to ¾	cup grated Swiss cheese
1	teaspoon all-purpose flour		¾	cup (more or less) finely chopped fresh parsley
3	tablespoons heavy cream			

MAKES 8 TO 10 SERVINGS

In a large skillet, melt the butter over medium-high heat. Sauté the onion and mushrooms until tender. Add the flour and reduce the heat to low. Cook for 3 minutes. Add the cream and stir until the mixture thickens. Season with salt and pepper. Cool completely.

Arrange the bread slices on a flat work surface. With a rolling pin, flatten the bread to

THE JOHN RUTLEDGE HOUSE BALLROOM

about ¼- to ⅛-inch thick. Spread each slice with a layer of the mushroom mixture. Sprinkle with grated cheese. Roll up each slice and wrap in plastic. Chill for at least 3 hours. Remove the plastic wrap and slice the mushroom rolls into ¼- to ¾-inch rounds. They will be a little moist and able to absorb a dipping of each round into the chopped parsley.

—JOHN RUTLEDGE HOUSE

Cranberry and Chicken Stuffed Nasturtium Blossoms

❧

Imagine trumpet-shaped garnet or persimmon-colored flowers holding a cranberry-chicken mixture, with teacups sitting beside the stuffed posies. Such an attractive finger food makes a striking addition to the tea table. Be sure the flowers have been washed well and stuff them carefully to keep the blooms intact. If nasturtiums are out of season, use the mixture for crackers or tea sandwiches. Jícama slices serve as edible coasters for the stuffed blossoms.

¹/₂	cup mayonnaise	3	drops Tabasco sauce
¹/₂	cup sour cream	40	nasturtium blossoms, cleaned
1	teaspoon salt	1	large jícama, peeled and sliced into ¹/₄-inch or thinner triangles
1	tablespoon minced green onions		
¹/₂	cup chopped dried cranberries		
1	cup finely chopped cooked chicken		

MAKES 40 SERVINGS

In a large bowl, combine the mayonnaise, sour cream, salt, onions, cranberries, chicken, and Tabasco sauce. Mix well.

Hold each nasturtium blossom by its base, and fill with a tablespoonful or so of the cranberry-chicken mixture. Arrange each stuffed blossom on a jícama triangle and serve.

—THE ALLEN HOUSE

Prosciutto, Fontina, and Sage Croque Monsieur

✎

The combination of cheese and ham, dipped in egg and then heated, makes this a croque-monsieur. (But the original croque monsieur, which was served in a Paris café in 1910, is made with Gruyère cheese and not dipped in the egg. An egg is served on top). You will love this version by Chef Phil McGrath.

6	slices white bread		3	eggs
6	thin slices prosciutto		3	tablespoons milk
6	ounces grated Fontina cheese			Freshly cracked black pepper
1	tablespoon fresh sage, cut julienne style			Butter for sautéing

MAKES 12 SERVINGS

*A*rrange 3 slices of bread on a flat surface. Cut 3 slices of prosciutto in half and place them on the bread slices. Sprinkle 2 ounces of cheese on each, then top with the sage. Cut the remaining pieces of prosciutto in half, and layer them over the cheese and sage. Top each slice with another piece of bread, pressing firmly to hold the filling in place. Trim and remove the crusts.

In a medium bowl, beat together the eggs and the milk. Season with freshly cracked black pepper.

Melt a tablespoon or so of butter in a skillet over medium heat. Dip each sandwich in the egg mixture and cook for a few minutes on each side, turning carefully, until the cheese melts and the bread is browned. To serve, cut the sandwiches into 4 triangles and serve warm.

—THE CASTLE AT TARRYTOWN

Maple-Glazed Ham, Leek, and Brie Sandwiches

⌇⌇⌇

Innkeeper Laura Simoes won a Jones Dairy Farm contest with this recipe. Jones offered bed-and-breakfast innkeepers a chance to compete for the best use of their products: all-natural ham, bacon, and sausage. Laura was one of the ten finalists in the country. I was one of the judges, and I could not get this sandwich out of my mind. Laura serves this at the inn for breakfast, but it is simply an adventure for tea-time.

CUT THESE SANDWICHES IN HALF AGAIN AND YOU'LL HAVE TEA-SIZE SANDWICHES.

2	large leeks (white parts only), cut lengthwise and then into 1/4-inch slices
2	tablespoons butter
2	tablespoons pure maple syrup
1/3	cup water
8	slices raisin bread
4	ounces Brie cheese, sliced
8	slices ham
2	tablespoons butter, melted

MAKES 16 TEA SANDWICHES

In a skillet, sauté the sliced leeks in butter for 2 to 3 minutes. Add the maple syrup and water. Simmer, uncovered, until the leeks are almost tender, about 2 to 3 minutes more. Assemble 4 sandwiches: top one slice of bread with 1 ounce of Brie, 2 slices of ham, and a portion of the leek mixture; top with another slice of bread. Brush both sides of the sandwich with melted butter. Grill on a preheated griddle until the bread is toasted and the cheese has melted. Slice each sandwich into 4 triangles.

—THE INN AT MAPLEWOOD FARM

There are many ways you can steep tea leaves. Many teapots now come with built-in infusers; otherwise, there are metal tea infusers for loose tea leaves that you dip into the teapot or cup; or just place the tea leaves into the teapot and let them steep, then filter through a strainer.

Rosemary and Chèvre Tea Sandwiches

✌◦✍

While enjoying tea at this fabulous castle, I had to write a postcard about the view I had just seen near the Hudson River. Then, to let the goat cheese melt in my mouth with this inventive sweet-and-savory sandwich, well, you'll just have to read the rest of my card someday.

12	1/4-inch-thick slices sour-dough baguette
4	tablespoons extra virgin olive oil
12	1/8-inch-thick slices goat cheese or Neufchâtel
1	bunch fresh rosemary, chopped (about 1 table-spoon),plus extra branches for garnish
18	yellow and/or red cherry tomatoes, chopped
	Salt
	Freshly cracked black pepper

MAKES 12 SERVINGS

*A*rrange the baguette slices on a baking sheet. Brush the bread with half the oil, and toast on both sides under a broiler until golden. Cool completely.

Top each with a slice of cheese and sprinkle with the chopped rosemary. Place the chopped tomatoes over the cheese and season with salt and pepper. Drizzle the sandwiches with the remaining olive oil and garnish with fresh rosemary branches. Serve at room temperature.

—THE CASTLE AT TARRYTOWN

*F*redericksburg Herb Farm innkeepers Bill and Sylvia Varney explain how to make a cup of fresh, hot herbal tea: Place 1 rounded teaspoon of the fresh herb into 1 cup of freshly boiled water. Steep for three to five minutes, depending on the strength of the herbal variety. Strain the herbs and enjoy the brew.

Shrimp, Tarragon, and Sweet Corn Cake Sandwiches

∽

Tea-time will never be the same with this interesting tea sandwich. The castle's chef is heralded for his creativity right down to afternoon tea.

WHIMSICAL CUPS AT AFTERNOON TEA GIVE GUESTS SOMETHING TO WRITE HOME ABOUT.

Corn Cakes

1	cup all-purpose flour
1/2	cup yellow or white cornmeal
1	tablespoon baking powder
1	tablespoon brown sugar
1/4	teaspoon salt
2	eggs
1 1/2	cups milk or buttermilk
	Butter for sautéing

Filling

2	tablespoons butter
12	medium shrimp, peeled and deveined
	Salt and freshly cracked black pepper
1	ear of corn, kernels removed
2	scallions, minced
1	tablespoon chopped tarragon
3	tablespoons crème fraîche (or sour cream)

MAKES 12 SERVINGS

*P*repare the corn cakes. In a mixing bowl, combine the flour, cornmeal, baking powder, sugar, and salt. In a separate bowl, stir together the eggs and the milk. Gradually add the dry ingredients to the egg mixture, mixing well after each addition.

In a large skillet, melt a tablespoon or so of butter over medium heat until it foams. Drop the batter by the tablespoonful into the hot skillet. Cook until bubbles begin to form. Turn the cakes and cook for an additional minute on the reverse side. Continue making cakes until the batter is used up, adding more butter to sauté as necessary. (You should have about 24 cakes.)

Prepare the sandwich filling. In a large skillet, melt the 2 tablespoons of butter over medium heat until it foams. Add the shrimp and cook for about 2 minutes, stirring occasionally. Season with salt and pepper. Add the corn and cook an additional 2 minutes. Add the scallions and the tarragon. Cook for about 30 seconds more, stirring well. Set the mixture aside to cool.

Remove the shrimp from the corn mixture. Arrange 2 corn cakes on individual plates. Place 2 of the cooled shrimp on a corn cake. Stir the crème fraîche into the corn mixture and scoop a generous portion over the shrimp. Top with the second corn cake to assemble the sandwiches. Cut each sandwich in half. Save any extra corn cakes for breakfast the next morning and serve with maple syrup.

—THE CASTLE AT TARRYTOWN

[51]

Tuna, Potato, and Green Onion on Rye

❧

Use Yukon Gold potatoes. Their buttery flavor adds to the creamy texture and taste of this sandwich. Serve the spread on rye bread or any intensely flavored bread.

1	6-ounce can white albacore tuna, drained	2	tablespoons mayonnaise
1/2	cup cold mashed potatoes	1	tablespoon minced red bell pepper
2	tablespoons finely chopped green onion	2	tablespoons minced celery

MAKES 1 1/2 CUPS

Combine all ingredients, mixing well. Spread on thinly sliced bread. Trim the crusts and carve into triangles. Serve immediately.

—ASA RANSOM HOUSE

Chicken, Capers, and Artichoke Sandwiches

❧

Our testers enjoyed adding cilantro and found the spread works well on pita bread. The petite nonpareil-size French caper is more difficult to chop, so use the larger Italian variety.

1	cup minced, cooked chicken	1/4	cup minced artichoke hearts
1/2	cup mayonnaise	1	teaspoon chopped fresh Italian parsley
2	tablespoons minced celery		Whole-wheat bread
1	tablespoon finely chopped capers		

MAKES 1 CUP

Combine all the ingredients, other than the bread, mixing well. Spread on thinly sliced whole-wheat bread. Trim the crusts and carve into triangles. Serve immediately.

—ASA RANSOM HOUSE

Grilled Mushroom and Herb Tea Sandwiches

∽∘∾

Cream cheese binds sautéed mushrooms and shallots and all is laced with herbs to make for a very special afternoon treat.

3	pounds button mushrooms, quartered		1/2	teaspoon finely chopped fresh rosemary
4	shallots, peeled and quartered		1/2	cup cream sherry
1/4	cup (1/2 stick) margarine		11/2	pounds cream cheese, cut into 1-inch pieces
	Salt		1	loaf firm white bread, sliced and crusts removed
	Freshly cracked black pepper			Butter for grilling
1	teaspoon dried thyme			
1	teaspoon dried savory			

MAKES 32 TEA SANDWICHES

In a food processor, coarsely chop the mushrooms and shallots, a few at a time so as not to chop too finely. Set aside.

Melt the margarine in a large sauté pan and cook the mushrooms and shallots over medium-low heat. Season with salt and pepper. Add the thyme, savory, rosemary, and sherry, and cook for 3 to 4 minutes, or until all the liquid has evaporated. Remove from the heat.

Stir the cream cheese into the mushroom mixture just to incorporate. Let the mixture stand until soft enough to thoroughly blend into a spreading consistency.

Spread the mixture on half of the bread slices. Place a slice of bread on top and lightly butter the outside of each sandwich. Grill until golden brown on both sides. Cut each sandwich into quarters and serve.

—INN AT GEORGIAN PLACE

*F*ruit and Vegetable Sandwiches on Raisin Bread

∽∾∾

A little bit of sweet and salty, smoothed out by the cream cheese, makes this an unforgettable sandwich and a perfect accompaniment to any afternoon tea. Cut the recipe according to your serving need.

2	8-ounce packages cream cheese, softened	1/4	cup finely chopped green bell pepper
8	ounces crushed pineapple, drained	1	tablespoon minced onion
1/3	cup orange marmalade	1/2	teaspoon celery salt
3	tablespoons ginger preserves or orange marmalade	1/2	teaspoon onion salt
1	cup finely chopped pecans	16	slices raisin bread

MAKES 64 BITE-SIZE SERVINGS

In a large bowl, combine the cream cheese, pineapple, marmalade, ginger preserves, 1/2 cup of the pecans, the green pepper, minced onion, celery salt, and onion salt. Mix well.

Halve the raisin bread slices on the diagonal and remove the crusts. Generously spread the fruit and vegetable mixture on the bread slices and top with the remaining pecans. Cut the sandwiches in half again.

—GAIL'S KITCHEN

In addition to herbs, tea may also be made from edible flowers with strong fragrances: marigolds, roses, hibiscus, chamomile, and jasmine. Dry the flowers. Pull the petals from the stems and spread out to dry on screens, away from sunlight. (To dry quickly, place petals in a 200-degree oven with the door ajar. Check every few minutes until they are crisp.) Steep a teaspoon of the dried petals into a cup of freshly boiled water for five to ten minutes and your tea is ready.

Pineapple, Sweet Red Pepper, and Mint Sandwiches

∽〇∾

It was unanimous. This refreshing spread is a real plus at tea-time with its minty taste. It goes well with almost anything else you serve.

8	ounces cream cheese, softened
¼	cup well-drained crushed pineapple
2	tablespoons minced red bell pepper
1	tablespoon fresh pineapple mint or spearmint
	Brown bread

MAKES 1 CUP

Combine all the ingredients except the bread, mixing well. Spread on thinly sliced brown bread. Trim the crusts and carve into triangles. Serve immediately.

—ASA RANSOM HOUSE

Find yourself an interesting, large basket for storing teas. It is okay to have several different varieties of tea from several different tea makers. I like certain tea makers, because I think they are good at real tea-leaf mixtures and others for their herbal flavors.

Tea-Filled Meatballs with Spicy Dipping Sauce

✺

Move over Swedish meatballs. Here comes a recipe that uses tea to flavor the meat. How appropriate for a high afternoon tea! The recipe comes from a book called *Cooking with Tea* by the folks at Celestial Seasonings tea makers. For best flavor, use Celestial Seasonings Herbal Spiced Tea.

Meatballs	
2	spiced herbal tea bags
2	tablespoons white vinegar
3	tablespoons water
1	pound quality ground pork
4	cloves garlic, minced
1	teaspoon dried oregano
1	teaspoon chili powder
1/2	teaspoon salt
1/2	cup crumbled Feta cheese
2	tablespoons olive oil for sautéing

Dipping Sauce	
1	spiced herbal tea bag
2	tablespoons white vinegar
1 1/2	cups sour cream
2	tablespoons water
1/2	teaspoon dried oregano
1/2	teaspoon freshly cracked black pepper

MAKES 6 SERVINGS

Prepare the meatballs. Steep the tea bags in the vinegar and cold water for 10 minutes. Combine the remaining ingredients in a large mixing bowl. Remove the tea bags from the liquid, squeeze the excess, and discard the bags. Add the tea mixture to the meat mixture and blend thoroughly. Form 12 to 15 meatballs.

Heat the oil in a large skillet over medium heat. Sauté the meatballs for 10 to 15 minutes, or until cooked through.

Prepare the dipping sauce. Steep the tea bag in cold vinegar for 10 minutes. Gently squeeze out the vinegar and discard the tea bag. Add the remaining ingredients and mix thoroughly. Serve with the meatballs.

—GAIL'S KITCHEN

Medieval High Tea Beef Pie

∾∾

Medieval cuisine is served almost nightly at this stately, three-year-old castle tucked between forest and farm in central Ohio. Meat pies were served all of the time in the days when castles were the homes of nobility.

This is high tea Ravenwood-Castle style. I like the addition of the parsley in the crust. Make your own brown gravy from the meat you prepare for the pie, or purchase a quality gravy.(Our testers found that frozen peas and carrots work well when fresh ones are not in season.)

GUARDING RAVENWOOD
CASTLE'S TEA-TIME SECRETS
IN THE MAIN DINING ROOM

Crust

2¹/₂	cups all-purpose flour
¹/₂	cup butter, softened
1	teaspoon chopped flat-leaf parsley
¹/₂	teaspoon salt
¹/₃ to ¹/₂	cup water, or enough to moisten

Filling

2	cups (about 1 pound raw) cooked steak, cut into 1-inch pieces
2	cups cooked ¹/₂-inch diced white potatoes (about 2 medium)
1	cup raw mixture small-dice of carrots and peas
1	cup or more brown gravy

Assembly

Light cream for brushing

MAKES 8 TO 10 SERVINGS

*B*egin by preparing the pastry crust. In a large mixing bowl, combine the flour, butter, parsley, and salt. Gradually incorporate enough water to form a pliable dough. Chill dough at least 4 hours. Remove from refrigerator and let sit 1 hour before continuing. Preheat the oven to 375°. Transfer the dough to a lightly floured surface; divide it into 2 sections. Roll out each section, creating ¹/₄-inch-thick circles. Carefully line a 10-inch pie plate with one of the circles.

Arrange the meat, potatoes, and vegetables in the pie shell. Add enough gravy to cover, and place the remaining pastry over the top, pinching the edges to seal. With a fork, prick the top crust in several places to ventilate while cooking. For a golden-brown finish, brush the surface with a coating of the light cream. Bake the pie for about 45 minutes, or until the crust has browned.

—RAVENWOOD CASTLE

Uncommon Confections

～∾～

Scottish Raspberry Buns

◡◠◡

This is an old, family heirloom recipe of the innkeeper, hence the term "buns." But these are actually sconelike in texture and have the appearance of a giant thumbprint cookie. The rice flour helps give the buns a more delicate texture.

1	cup all-purpose flour
3/4	cup rice flour (or substitute with 1 cup all-purpose flour)
1/2	teaspoon baking powder
1/8	teaspoon salt
1/4	cup sugar
4	tablespoons butter
1/4	cup whole milk, tepid
1	egg
8 to 10	teaspoons raspberry jam (about 1/3 cup)

MAKES 8 BUNS

Preheat the oven to 400°. In a medium mixing bowl, sift together the flours, baking powder, salt, and sugar. Cut in the butter until coarse crumbs form.

In a separate bowl, stir together the milk and the egg. Add the liquid to the dry ingredients and blend until a dough forms.

Form 8 uniform-size balls, about 1½ inches each, and place them on an ungreased baking sheet. Using a knife, indent each ball and fill with about 1 teaspoon of raspberry jam. Bake for 12 to 15 minutes, or until lightly browned.

—TRILLIUM

I have several teapots in my collection, and I keep many of them in my office where I can see them every day and think of the pleasures and treasures they can hold.

English Toffee Shortbread with Chocolate Frosting

❦

A chocolate topping tucks in a sumptuous toffee filling that is spread over buttery shortbread. No one walks away disappointed with this one.

Shortbread

1/2	cup all-purpose flour
1/4	teaspoon baking powder
1/4	cup sugar
1/4	cup (1/2 stick) butter, softened

Topping

1/4	cup (1/2 stick) butter
2	tablespoons light-grade (golden) maple syrup
1/2	cup sugar
1	cup sweetened condensed milk
2	8-ounce quality chocolate bars, melted

MAKES 8 TO 10 SERVINGS

*P*reheat the oven to 350°. Combine the flour, baking powder, and sugar in a medium mixing bowl. Cut in the butter until coarse crumbs form. Gently flatten the dough into a lightly greased 8-inch square baking pan. Bake for 15 minutes or until golden. Remove the shortbread from the oven and let cool while preparing the toffee topping.

In a medium saucepan, combine the butter, syrup, sugar, and condensed milk. Bring to a boil and simmer for 5 to 10 minutes. Remove from the heat and set aside.

Pour the toffee mixture over the top. Cool completely so that it hardens slightly. Melt the chocolate over a double boiler until spreading consistency. Spread a layer of the chocolate overtop the caramel filling. Cut the shortbread into 1-inch or 2-inch squares, as desired.

—BETSY'S BED & BREAKFAST

*T*ea for one is an adventure I look forward to whenever I need a soothing moment alone. I set a small tray with tea equipage for myself: either a lace doily or a piece of homespun, a favorite teacup, a small teapot that a friend gave me, a little pitcher of milk and a cookie or a piece of cake. I may be in my jeans in the midst of a hectic workday, but the sight of my tea tray always relieves stress and reminds me to enjoy the little things.

*L*emon Shortbread Baked in a Pie Plate

◈

The lemon in this traditional cookie makes this shortbread even more amenable to a cup of tea. And its comforting taste doesn't distract you as you take bites and write a little more on that postcard to a friend.

Crust		*Filling*	
1	cup sugar	2	eggs
2	cups all-purpose flour	1	cup sugar
3/4	cup (1 1/2 sticks) cold butter, cut into small pieces	1/4	cup freshly squeezed lemon juice
			Grated peel from 1 orange

MAKES 8 TO 10 SERVINGS

*P*reheat the oven to 350°. Prepare the crust. Mix together the sugar and the flour in a large mixing bowl. Cut in the butter and blend with your fingertips until coarse crumbs form.

Press the crumbs into a greased 9-inch pie plate. Bake for 15 minutes, or until golden. Turn the oven down to 325°.

Meanwhile, prepare the filling. Combine the eggs, sugar, and lemon juice in a mixing bowl. Beat well by hand. Pour the mixture over the prepared crust. Bake for 15 to 20 minutes. Sprinkle the pie with orange peel while still hot. Refrigerate the shortbread until set. Slice into wedges and serve.

VIEW FROM THE PARLOR ON THE PAULINE

—THE *PAULINE*

Orange Saffron Pound Cake with Orange Custard Sauce

∽∾∾

Saffron, the yellow-orange stigmas from a small purple crocus, is the world's most expensive spice. It takes about 14,000 strands of these stigmas to make an ounce of saffron. Pungent and aromatic, saffron flavors and colors food. But here's a little secret. I find that the edible petals of calendula flowers will give the same color and a similar taste for a lot less expense. This cake from the castle has a totally royal taste.

Cake		Sauce	
1	cup buttermilk	3	egg yolks
5 to 7	strands saffron (or 2 table-spoons calendula petals)	1²/₃	cups milk
1¹/₂	cups butter, softened	3	tablespoons all-purpose flour
3	cups sugar	1	cup sugar
5	eggs	1	teaspoon orange extract
2	teaspoons vanilla extract	2	tablespoons grated orange peel or more, for garnish.
3¹/₃	cups sifted cake flour		
¹/₂	teaspoon baking powder		
¹/₃	cup grated orange peel, plus extra for garnish		

MAKES 8 TO 10 SERVINGS

*P*reheat the oven to 300°. Measure the buttermilk into a small bowl. Add the saffron strands and set aside. In a mixing bowl, combine the butter and sugar. Beat at high speed until light and fluffy. Add the eggs, one at a time, beating thoroughly after each addition. Add the vanilla.

In a separate bowl, combine the flour, baking powder, and orange peel. Alternately add the dry ingredients and the saffron/buttermilk mixture to the butter mixture in 3 batches, beating well after each addition.

Pour the batter into a greased and floured 10-inch tube pan. Bake for 1 hour and 45 minutes, or until the top is golden and a tester comes clean. Cool the cake on a wire rack for 15 minutes before removing from the pan.

Meanwhile, prepare the custard sauce. In a medium saucepan, whisk the egg yolks and ²/₃ cup of the milk over medium heat. Combine the flour and the sugar in a small bowl. Add to the saucepan, whisking constantly over medium heat until all ingredients are well blended. Add the remaining 1 cup of milk, and mix well until the custard thickens. Remove the pan from the heat, and stir in the orange extract. Serve the sauce, warm or chilled, over the top of the pound cake. Garnish with grated orange peel.

—RAVENWOOD CASTLE

The warmth of afternoon tea by the hearth at the Captain Swift Inn in Camden, Maine

Poppy Seed Pound Cake with Orange Glaze

Poppy seed cakes go well with tea-time beverages. I like this cake with the tangy flavor of the orange.

Cake

3	eggs
1½	cups milk
1	cup vegetable oil
1½	teaspoons vanilla extract
½	teaspoon almond extract
1½	teaspoons baking powder
½	teaspoon salt
2¼	cups sugar
3	cups all-purpose flour
2	tablespoons poppy seeds

Glaze

6	tablespoons sugar
2	tablespoons freshly squeezed orange juice
¼	teaspoon vanilla extract
⅛	teaspoon almond extract

MAKES 8 TO 10 SERVINGS

Preheat the oven to 350°. In a large mixing bowl, combine the eggs, milk, oil, and extracts. Mix well. Add the baking powder, salt, sugar, flour, and poppy seeds. Beat for about 2 minutes, until the mixture is well combined. Spoon the batter into a greased and floured bundt pan, or 2 small bundt pans. Bake for 50 to 60 minutes, or until a tester comes clean. Cool the cake in its pan for about 5 minutes. Remove from the pan and cool completely on a wire rack. Meanwhile, prepare the glaze. Combine the sugar, orange juice, vanilla, and almond extract in a small saucepan. Bring the mixture to a boil, stirring constantly. Reduce the heat and simmer for 1 to 2 minutes. Drizzle over cooled pound cake.

—CAPTAIN SWIFT INN

Whole-Wheat Pound Cake

⌘

I like to keep this cake on hand for those times when I take afternoon tea-for-one. It freezes well and includes a little less in the way of guilt-ridden ingredients thanks to the whole-wheat flour. Innkeeper Kathy Filip tells me that you may also frost this cake with your favorite icing.

1	cup (2 sticks) margarine
3	cups sugar
6	eggs
1	cup sour cream
1	teaspoon vanilla extract
1	teaspoon almond extract
1/4	teaspoon baking soda
2	cups all-purpose flour
1	cup whole-wheat flour

MAKES 8 TO 10 SERVINGS

Preheat the oven to 350°. In a mixing bowl, cream together the margarine and the sugar until smooth. Add the eggs, 1 at a time, beating well after each addition. Add the sour cream, extracts, baking soda, and flours. Stir well.

Pour the batter into a greased and floured bundt pan, or 2 small bundt pans. Bake for 60 to 65 minutes. Cool the cake in the pan for 8 to 10 minutes, then remove from the pan and cool completely on a wire rack.

—CAPTAIN SWIFT INN

Here's a simple pleasure: Find yourself a hat shop—there are two of them within an hour's driving time of my home. One is the Proper Topper in Washington D.C.'s marble-and-brass renovated old depot, Union Station, and the other is Hats in the Belfry in Annapolis, Maryland's charming historic waterfront town. When I'm a little down, I go into one of these shops and try on the season's latest chapeaus. Stress and problems give way to smiles and once in a while I buy something and wear the hat to my next afternoon tea. Try the nearest clothing store if you don't have a hat boutique nearby.

B*rownie Pound Cake*

Although a brownie in taste, this actually cuts like a cake. It is the best chocolate pound cake I have ever tasted. Frost with your favorite chocolate icing or simply glaze, using the method below.

Cake

1	cup (2 sticks) margarine
3	cups sugar
4	eggs
1	cup sour cream
1/2	cup oil
1/2	cup brewed coffee, chilled
1/2	teaspoon baking powder
1/2	teaspoon salt
1/2	cup powdered unsweetened cocoa
3	cups all-purpose flour
1	cup mini-chocolate chips

Glaze

3	tablespoons milk
1/2	teaspoon butter extract
1/2	teaspoon vanilla extract
1	cup powdered sugar

MAKES 8 TO 10 SERVINGS

*P*reheat the oven to 300°. Cream together the margarine and the sugar until smooth. Add the eggs, 1 at a time, beating well after each addition. Beat in the sour cream, oil, and coffee. Add the baking powder, salt, cocoa, and flour, stirring well. Fold in the chocolate chips.

Pour the batter into a greased and floured bundt pan, or 2 small bundt pans. Bake for 50 to 60 minutes, or until a tester comes clean. Cool the cake in its pan for 8 to 10 minutes, then remove from the pan and cool completely on a wire rack.

Meanwhile, prepare the glaze. Combine the milk, extracts, and sugar in a mixing bowl. Stir until smooth and spread over the cooled pound cake.

—CAPTAIN SWIFT INN

Java Chip Bundt Cake with Vanilla Icing

෴

A cake and a pudding mix help speed this delicious cake along, especially for last-minute company.

Cake		Icing	
1	package chocolate cake mix	3	tablespoons milk
1	small package instant chocolate pudding	1/2	teaspoon butter extract
		1/2	teaspoon vanilla extract
1	cup sour cream	1	cup powdered sugar
1/2	cup vegetable oil		
1/2	cup brewed coffee		
4	eggs, beaten		
1	cup mini-chocolate chips		

MAKES 8 TO 10 SERVINGS

Preheat the oven to 350°. In a large bowl, combine the cake mix, instant pudding, sour cream, oil, coffee, and eggs. Mix well. Stir in the chocolate chips.

Pour the batter into a greased and floured bundt pan, or 2 small bundt pans. Bake for 50 to 60 minutes, or until a tester comes clean. Cool the cake in the pan for 8 to 10 minutes, then turn out and cool completely on a wire rack.

Meanwhile, prepare the icing. In a large bowl, combine the milk, butter extract, vanilla, and sugar, stirring until smooth. Drizzle over the cooled bundt cake.

—CAPTAIN SWIFT INN

Here is something you can write on a postcard while sipping tea. It is a quote I found on a greeting card and is attributed to an ancient Chinese prophet: "Here at the frontier, there are falling leaves; although my neighbors are barbarians, and you, you are a thousand miles away. . . . There are always two cups at my table."

Chocolate Swirl Cake with Chocolate Glaze

❧

Swirled cake is a pretty addition to the table. To accomplish this easy artistry, it takes a little back-and-forth work with parts of the cake batter made in several bowls.

Cake

1¹/₂	cups (3 sticks) butter, at room temperature
3	cups sugar
5	eggs
3¹/₂	cups sifted cake flour
¹/₂	teaspoon baking powder
1	cup buttermilk
2	teaspoons vanilla extract
¹/₂	cup powdered unsweetened cocoa

Glaze

1¹/₂	cups semisweet chocolate morsels
4	tablespoons butter
1	tablespoon vanilla extract

MAKES 8 TO 10 SERVINGS

*P*reheat the oven to 300°. Grease and flour a 10-inch tube pan. In the bowl of an electric mixer, beat the butter and sugar until light and fluffy. Add the eggs, 1 at a time, beating well after each addition.

In a separate bowl, combine the flour and the baking powder. In a small bowl, combine the buttermilk and the vanilla. Add the flour mixture to the butter-sugar mixture, alternating with the buttermilk-vanilla mixture. Beat thoroughly after each addition.

Ladle half of the batter into a clean bowl. Beat the cocoa into one of the bowls. Ladle, into the tube pan, half the vanilla cake batter and half the chocolate batter. Repeat with remaining batters. Cut through the batters to create a swirl pattern by passing the knife through the batters in a swirl motion. Bake for 1 hour 45 minutes, or until a tester comes clean.

Prepare the chocolate glaze. Combine the chocolate and the butter in a microwave dish. Cook on high until melted, about 2 minutes. Add the vanilla and beat until smooth. Immediately drizzle the warm glaze over the cake.

—RAVENWOOD CASTLE

LEFT: THE CHOCOLATE SWIRL CAKE TAKES THE CROWNING POSITION

Rhubarb and Berry Sour Cream Nut Cake ✓

❧

Consider this recipe a basket of berries in a cake. It is a moist and interesting cake, perfect for tea. If you cannot find rhubarb in season, substitute peaches or plums, or double up on the berries. Our testers also made this successfully in a bundt pan, baked in a 325° oven for 1 hour and 45 minutes.

1	cup (2 sticks) butter, softened	1½	cups sour cream
2	cups sugar	1	tablespoon vanilla extract
4	eggs	2	cups fresh blueberries
4	cups all-purpose flour, plus more for coating	1	cup fresh raspberries
4	teaspoons baking powder	1	cup finely diced rhubarb
1	teaspoon salt	1½	cups chopped walnuts
			Cinnamon sugar

MAKES 24 TEA-TIME SERVINGS

*P*reheat the oven to 350°. In a mixing bowl, cream the butter and sugar until light and fluffy. Add the eggs, 1 at a time, beating well after each addition. In a separate bowl, combine the 4 cups of flour, baking powder, and salt. In a small bowl, mix together the sour cream and vanilla.

Alternately add the flour mixture and the sour cream mixture to the butter–sugar mixture. Blend until just combined. Gently toss the fruit in the remaining flour and fold into the batter.

Pour the batter into a greased and floured 13x9-inch pan. Sprinkle with chopped walnuts and cinnamon sugar. Bake for 30 minutes, or until a tester comes clean.

—THE ALLEN HOUSE

*P*lum and Nectarine Crisp

∽◌∾

A light, fruit confection such as this dish, would go particularly well with an herbal tea or the brandied café drink on page 9. It also goes well with a serving of whipped cream or ice cream. Our testers added oats to this recipe for added texture. (You may substitute 6 small pears and 2 large Granny Smith apples for the fruit.)

Topping			
3/4	cup unbleached all-purpose flour	4	medium nectarines, pitted and cut into 1/8- to 1/4-inch slices
1/4	cup old-fashioned oats	1/2	cup packed light brown sugar
1/2	cup sugar	1/8	teaspoon ground cloves
1/4	cup (1/2 stick) butter	1	teaspoon cinnamon
1	teaspoon cinnamon	1	teaspoon tapioca (or flour if fruit is very juicy)
Filling			
6	medium purple or red plums, pitted and cut into 1/8- to 1/4-inch slices		

MAKES 8 SERVINGS

*P*reheat the oven to 350°. Combine all of the topping ingredients in a large mixing bowl. Using your fingers or a pastry blender, work the mixture into an even consistency.

In a separate bowl, combine the fruit slices, sugar, cloves, cinnamon, and tapioca, mixing gently. Transfer the filling to a 13x9-inch glass baking dish. Sprinkle the topping evenly over the fruit, pressing the crumbs lightly. Bake for 30 minutes, or until the top is lightly browned. Serve warm or at room temperature.

—AMADEUS HOUSE

Sweet Prune Cakes with Buttermilk Vanilla Sauce

∽○∾

In the mini-bundt shape, these cakes look elegant, one to a plate—like little jeweled crowns. When I tasted these at the inn, I couldn't believe they contained prunes. Each tea-time guest may be served an individual prune cake.

Cakes

2	cups sugar
3/4	cup vegetable oil
3	eggs, beaten
1	teaspoon vanilla extract
1	cup buttermilk
2	cups all-purpose flour
1	teaspoon baking powder
1	teaspoon baking soda
1/2	teaspoon salt
1	teaspoon cinnamon
1	teaspoon nutmeg
1	teaspoon allspice
1	cup pitted baby prunes, finely chopped

Sauce

1/2	cup sugar
1/4	cup buttermilk
1/2	cup (1 stick) butter
1	teaspoon vanilla extract

MAKES 10 CAKES

*P*reheat the oven to 300°. In a medium bowl, combine the sugar, oil, eggs, vanilla, and buttermilk. Mix well. In a large bowl, whisk together the flour, baking powder, baking soda, salt, and spices. Add the buttermilk mixture to the dry ingredients, stirring well. Fold in the prunes.

Pour the batter into 10 mini-bundt cups, about 3/4 full. Bake 35 to 40 minutes, or until cakes spring back when touched. Cool on a wire rack for about 45 minutes. Invert the pans onto a cookie sheet. Wait 10 minutes before removing the bundt pans to release the cakes.

To prepare the sauce, combine all the ingredients in a double boiler. Cook until warm and thoroughly combined. Pour over cakes.

—THE DAVY JACKSON INN

In the dell in our garden my dolls and I take tea, and days when I have raisins the catbirds dine with me. —Elizabeth Merrill from a greeting card of artist Susan Branch

Spiced Tea Cake with Raspberry Filling and Chocolate Frosting

༄

Years ago, the country store down by the lake sold frosted spice cakes, which my friends and I bought to eat on the walk home from the school bus. I must admit this version, incorporating raspberry preserves and icing, beats by a long shot the over-the-counter treats we thought were so heavenly. Whipped with cream and chocolate, this frosting is lighter than most—perfect for afternoon tea.

Cake

1½	cups all-purpose flour
½	teaspoon baking soda
2	teaspoons ground ginger
1	teaspoon cinnamon
¼	teaspoon ground cloves
¼	teaspoon allspice
½	cup buttermilk
2	teaspoons vanilla extract
½	cup (1 stick) unsalted butter
½	cup packed light brown sugar
½	cup unsulfured light molasses
1	teaspoon grated orange peel
2	eggs

Frosting

¾	cup heavy cream
¾	cup sugar
3	ounces unsweetened chocolate, chopped
5	tablespoons unsalted butter
¾	teaspoon vanilla extract
⅛	teaspoon salt

Filling

⅓	cup raspberry preserves

MAKES 10 TO 12 SERVINGS

*P*reheat the oven to 350°. Grease and flour an 8-inch round cake pan.

In a large bowl, whisk together the flour, baking soda, ginger, cinnamon, cloves, and allspice. Set aside. In a separate bowl, combine the buttermilk and the vanilla. In large bowl of electric mixer, cream together the butter and brown sugar until light and fluffy. Beat in the molasses, orange peel, and then the eggs, 1 at a time, beating well after each addition. Add the flour mixture alternately with the buttermilk mixture, beating well after each addition. Spread the batter evenly in the prepared pan. Bake for 35 to 40 minutes, or until a tester comes clean. Invert the cake onto a wire rack and cool completely.

Meanwhile, prepare the frosting. In a small saucepan, bring the cream and sugar to a boil. Reduce the heat to low and simmer, stirring occasionally, until the liquid has reduced by about a fourth. In a large mixing bowl, combine the cream mixture, chocolate, butter, vanilla, and salt. Stir until the chocolate and butter have melted. Place the mixing bowl inside a larger bowl filled with ice water. Stir frequently over the ice until cooled, about 12 minutes. Beat the frosting with an electric mixer until thick and fluffy.

With a long, serrated knife, cut the cake in half horizontally. Arrange the bottom layer , cut side up, on a cake plate. Spread with raspberry preserves. Cover the preserves with the remaining cake layer, cut side down. Spread the frosting around the entire cake.

—GAIL'S KITCHEN

Raspberry and Toasted Almond Bread Pudding with Caramel Sauce

ᴄᴏᴏ

Put a bread pudding out with your choice of tea sweets and it will go every time. I had never had one with raspberries. But when I did, I had to have the recipe. I remember tasting this special bread pudding with raspberries in the tea room on the castle grounds, while I was taking a leisurely work break. Making it at home brings me right back to the castle. If you do not have your own raspberry muffin recipe, see the one on page 104.

Pudding

12	day-old raspberry muffins
2 to 3	cups milk
7	eggs
1/2	cup white sugar
3/4	cup light brown sugar
1	cup toasted, coarsely chopped almonds, plus extra for garnish
1	teaspoon nutmeg
1 1/2	teaspoons almond extract
1 3/4	cups fresh or frozen raspberries, plus extra for garnish

Sauce

1/2	cup butter
1/2	cup sugar
1/2	cup packed brown sugar
1/2	cup heavy cream
1 1/2	teaspoons vanilla extract

MAKES 12 SERVINGS

*P*reheat the oven to 350°. Break the muffins into small pieces and place them into a large mixing bowl. Slowly pour 2 cups of the milk over the muffins until the liquid is absorbed. Continue adding milk until the muffins are moist.

Beat the eggs in a separate bowl until smooth. Add the white sugar, brown sugar, almonds, nutmeg, and extract, beating well. When the mixture is thoroughly combined, stir in the milk-soaked muffins, then the raspberries. Ladle the batter into 12 lightly greased 3- to 3 1/2-inch ramekins. Bake for 45 to 50 minutes, or until the centers are set. Invert puddings onto individual serving plates.

Prepare the caramel sauce. In a small saucepan, combine the butter, white sugar, brown sugar, heavy cream, and vanilla extract. Whisk over medium-low heat until the butter melts. Gradually increase heat until the sauce comes to a boil. Continue boiling for 1 minute. Remove the saucepan from the heat and whisk until the foam disappears. Drizzle the warm sauce over the bread puddings. Garnish with raspberries and toasted almonds.

—RAVENWOOD CASTLE

Peanut Butter Cheesecake with Chocolate Glaze

୨୦୬

It is a treat sitting in the tea room at the castle, enjoying this lush dessert. I just had to have the recipe. Be sure your oven is reading 300° so that the cake cooks properly and according to directions. Note: Add a tablespoon or two more of butter to thin the glaze.

Crust

1½	cups graham cracker crumbs
2	tablespoons melted butter
1	tablespoon sugar

Cheesecake

3	8-ounce packages cream cheese, at room temperature
1	cup sugar
½	cup crunchy or smooth peanut butter

1	teaspoon vanilla extract
4	eggs

Glaze

2	tablespoons butter
2	tablespoons chocolate chips or grated semisweet chocolate
2	teaspoons vanilla extract

MAKES 10 TO 12 SERVINGS

Prepare the crust. In a large bowl, combine the cracker crumbs, melted butter, and sugar. Sprinkle the crumb mixture evenly over the bottom of a greased (preferably nonstick) 10-inch springform pan. Set aside.

Preheat the oven to 300°. Prepare the filling. In a large mixing bowl, beat together the cream cheese, sugar, peanut butter, and vanilla. When the mixture is smooth, add the eggs, one at a time. Beat for about 1 minute after each addition, scraping the sides of the bowl frequently. Once all the eggs are incorporated, beat the mixture for another 2 to 3 minutes, or until very smooth and fluffy.

Pour the batter into the prepared pan. Bake for 45 minutes, then turn off the oven, but do not open the door. Allow the cake to stand for 20 to 30 minutes inside. Remove the cake from the oven and cool in the pan completely.

Meanwhile, prepare the chocolate glaze. In a small saucepan, melt the butter and chocolate over medium heat. Transfer the mixture to a bowl and stir in the vanilla. Beat until smooth. Drizzle the chocolate over the cooled cheesecake.

—RAVENWOOD CASTLE

Tea-Time Pantry

〜∞〜

Even a mountain-sized portion of this Sundried Tomato Paté is never enough.

Picture facing chapter opener: Tea leaves and tea-time spreads—Peach Chutney, Sundried Tomato Paté, and Cucumber and Basil Cheese Spread

Sundried Tomato Pâté

∽∘∾

Put out the water crackers or the sourdough bread and serve this delicious pâté with one of the non-tea beverages suggested in the "Saucer's Apprentice" chapter. You will need to begin preparation of the pâté about four hours ahead of serving time.

½	cup sundried tomatoes, packed in oil	1	clove garlic
8	ounces cream cheese	¼	teaspoon oregano
¼	cup (½ stick) butter	½	teaspoon rosemary
½	cup grated Parmesan cheese	¼	teaspoon basil

MAKES 1½ CUPS

Combine all ingredients in a food processor. Blend well, pausing frequently to scrape the sides. Refrigerate at least 4 hours before serving.

—THE IDAHO COUNTRY INN

I recently discovered a great addition for my tea table: spoon rests. These small silver coasters keep a wet teaspoon from staining a dainty tablecloth. Saucers provide a place to set a spoon for hot tea, but that can be cumbersome, and besides, tea is often served in mugs these days. And what do you do about iced tea spoons? The coasters are sold by mail order from Camellia & Main (1-800-929-9494.) The catalog maintains they are a reproduction of antebellum spoon rests.

"*Sip and let the world boil down to just this cup, this moment, and let the warmth slowly spread from your fingers throughout your whole body to your soul. Reflect, analyze, dream, and plan. For now, the world is right here.*"
—*Alexandra Stoddard from* Tea Celebrations

Cucumber and Basil Cheese Spread

∽○∾

About as refreshing as a spring afternoon, this spread can be sandwiched between rye or pumpernickel breads or more exotic savory breads. It is also great with crackers. The spread needs two hours in the refrigerator to rest before serving.

1/2	cup mayonnaise
1/4	cup sour cream
1/4	cup ranch-style dressing
1/2	cup cream cheese, softened
1/4	teaspoon curly-leaf parsley
1/4	teaspoon minced fresh basil

1/2	teaspoon salt
1/2	teaspoon freshly cracked black pepper
1/2	cup peeled, seeded, and finely diced cucumbers

MAKES 2 CUPS

In a large mixing bowl, cream together all of the ingredients except the cucumbers. When the mixture is smooth, stir in the diced cucumbers. Cover and chill for 2 hours.

—JOHN RUTLEDGE HOUSE

Do not just wait for when you are away to send a postcard to a friend. Sometimes, we hesitate to write because we think we have to send long letters. Getting a postcard from you is an uplifting experience letting your receiver know they are thought of and missed.

Cheesy Crab Dip

୶୦ଊ

Something about crab dips and tea-time go together, perhaps because tea-time is often hors d'oeuvre time. Crab is a delicate seafood and when dressed with lemon juice and hot sauce, crab has an interesting mix of flavors, one accenting the other. Serve the dip with water crackers and plan to make a few hours ahead of serving time.

½	cup mayonnaise	2	tablespoons finely chopped chives
½	cup cream cheese, softened	2	cups lump crab meat
½	cup ranch-style dressing		Salt
1	tablespoon fresh lemon juice		Freshly cracked black pepper
1	teaspoon Worcestershire sauce	1	cup shredded Cheddar cheese
½	teaspoon hot sauce		

MAKES 4 CUPS

In a large mixing bowl, cream together the mayonnaise, cream cheese, ranch dressing, lemon juice, Worcestershire, and hot sauce. When the mixture is thoroughly combined, stir in the chives and crab meat. Season with salt and pepper. Gently fold in the Cheddar cheese. Cover and chill for 3 hours before serving.

—JOHN RUTLEDGE HOUSE

LEFT: THE JOHN RUTLEDGE HOUSE, BEAUFORT, SOUTH CAROLINA

Smoked Trout Dip

∽◌∾

Many folks enjoy the flavor of smoky trout; and combined with the hot sauce and the tangy dill, the dip will be sought after by your partygoers. This is nice served on plain crackers.

1	smoked trout (about 4 ounces)	2	tablespoons lemon juice
4	ounces cream cheese, softened	1/4	teaspoon Tabasco sauce
1/4	cup finely diced yellow onion		Fresh mint for garnish
1/8	teaspoon dill		
1/4	teaspoon Worcestershire sauce		

MAKES 1 CUP

Remove the skin and filet the trout. Flake into small pieces. In a mixing bowl, beat the cream cheese, onion, dill, Worcestershire sauce, lemon juice, and Tabasco sauce until smooth. Stir in the trout. Place in a bowl and garnish with mint.

—THE IDAHO COUNTRY INN

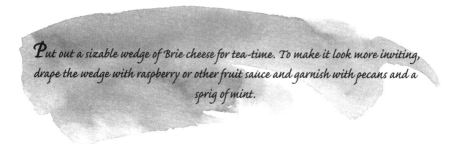

Put out a sizable wedge of Brie cheese for tea-time. To make it look more inviting, drape the wedge with raspberry or other fruit sauce and garnish with pecans and a sprig of mint.

P*lum Conserve*

❧❧❧

A plum condiment is an elegant addition to a tea setting. Serve with graham crackers and cream cheese.

5	cups (about 2 pounds) fresh plums, sliced
2	cups honey
1/2	cup finely chopped fresh lemon, with peel
1	cup raisins
1/2	cup slivered almonds
4	half-pint jelly jars, with lids and rings, prepared for hot water processing

MAKES 4 CUPS

In a heavy Dutch oven set over medium-high heat, combine the plum slices and the honey. Stir in the chopped lemon and the raisins. Bring to a boil. Cook for about 15 to 25 minutes (depending on juiciness of plums), stirring frequently, until the mixture has thickened. Remove from the heat and stir in the almonds. Fill hot, half-pint jars with the plum mixture to within 1/4 inch of the tops. Place a lid on each jar and band loosely. Process for about 10 minutes in a boiling water bath. Remove the jars from the water bath and tighten the bands. Cool completely.

—TRILLIUM

Beach Plum Jelly

Beach plums grow close to the shore, especially on Cape Cod, in thick bushes four to five feet high. The plum, as it ripens, changes from green to red, and then deep purple. The less ripe plums contain more pectin than the ripe ones, so be sure to include both in a proportion of about 1 cup green to 4 cups red plums. Incorporate the jelly with the rose petal scones recipe on page 32.

1	cup green beach plums
4	cups red beach plums
	Sugar

MAKES 4 CUPS

Wash the plums and remove the stems. Place the fruit in an enamel pot and add enough water to cover. Bring to a boil, drain, and discard the water. Return the plums to the pot and add enough boiling water to barely cover. Cook until soft, occasionally mashing the plums with a wooden spoon. Turn the fruit and juice into a jelly bag made of several thicknesses of cheesecloth suspended over a large bowl. Allow the mixture to drain overnight, or until all the juice drips through. Do not squeeze the bag, or the jelly will be clouded.

Measure the juice into a large saucepan. For each cup of juice, add 1 cup of sugar. Bring the mixture to a boil over medium-high heat and cook until the juice "sheets." (The mixture will drip off a spoon in 2 drops that run together and fall from the spoon in a sheet.) Remove from the heat, skim the surface if necessary, and pour the mixture into sterile jelly jars. Seal with 2 layers of melted paraffin and lids. Store in a cool, dark place.

—THE WILDFLOWER INN

Ginger Peach Chutney

~∞~

4	pounds fresh peaches, peeled, pitted, and sliced	1	onion, chopped
1	cup raisins	1	teaspoon mustard seed
1	cup fresh lime juice	1	tablespoon celery seed
1	cup white vinegar	1	tablespoon chopped, crystallized ginger
3	green chili peppers, chopped	1½	tablespoons salt
3	cloves garlic, minced	1	pound dark brown sugar

MAKES 4 PINTS

Combine all of the ingredients in a large casserole. Bring to a boil. Reduce the heat and simmer, stirring occasionally, for 3 hours. Ladle the mixture into sterilized jars, filling to within ¼ inch of the tops. Wipe the jar rims and seal. Process the chutney in a boiling water bath for 10 minutes. Drain, check seals, and store in a cool, dark place

—GAIL'S KITCHEN

Make a healthy cup of ginger tea. Steep 1 teaspoon of freshly grated ginger in a cup of boiled water. Let steep 5 minutes. Strain and add a teaspoon or more of honey.

Citrus Sorbet with Ginger Lime Sauce

∽◦∾

I haven't ever seen sorbet served at afternoon tea, but what a splendid idea. During tea, you are eating such an assortment of tastes that it's nice to have a palate cleanser.

Sorbet	
4	cups sugar
4	cups water
1¹/₂	cups cold freshly squeezed citrus juice (lemon, lime, or orange)

Ginger Lime Sauce	
¹/₂	cup sugar
¹/₂	cup packed brown sugar
6	tablespoons water
¹/₄	cup fresh lime juice
2	tablespoons chopped, crystallized ginger
3	tablespoons unsalted butter

MAKES 4 CUPS

To make the sorbet, combine the sugar and water in a large saucepan and bring to a boil. Simmer for 5 to 6 minutes, or until the sugar dissolves—do not stir. Cool completely.

Combine 1 cup of the sugar syrup with the citrus juice and process in an electric ice-cream maker for 25 minutes. Immediately transfer the sorbet to a plastic container and store in the freezer until ready to serve.

Prepare the sauce. In a heavy-bottomed saucepan, combine all the sauce ingredients. Stir over low heat until the sugar dissolves. Bring to a boil and cook for about 15 minutes, or until the liquid is reduced to 1 cup.

Serve the sorbet in glass dessert dishes; drizzle with lime sauce.

—THE ALLEN HOUSE

Buttermint Cookies

Tea-time is complete with a serving of these tried-and-true mint-flavored butter cookies.

3/4	cup unsalted butter, softened
2/3	cup sugar
1	egg, beaten lightly
1/2	teaspoon vanilla extract
1	teaspoon peppermint extract

1/2	teaspoon orange extract
2	cups all-purpose flour, sifted
2	tablespoons minced fresh peppermint leaves
1/8	teaspoon salt

MAKES 4 DOZEN

In bowl of an electric mixer, cream the butter with the sugar. Slowly beat in the egg and the extracts. Beat until the mixture is light and fluffy. Add the flour—a little at a time. Then add the peppermint leaves and salt. Beat until thouroughly combined. Divide the dough into 3 parts. Form each part into a log about 1¼ inches in diameter. Wrap each dough log in plastic, then chill for 1 hour, or place in the freezer for 15 to 20 minutes.

Preheat the oven to 350°. Slice the dough into rounds about ¼-inch thick and arrange them on baking sheets about 1 inch apart. Bake for 10 to 12 minutes, or until light gold. Cool on wire racks.

THE MERRY SHERWOOD PLANTATION, NOT FAR FROM THE OCEAN ON MARYLAND'S BUCOLIC EASTERN SHORE

—MERRY SHERWOOD PLANTATION INN

[103]

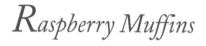

Raspberry Muffins

The delicious caramel pudding (see page 86) calls for raspberry muffins, so here is a recipe to help us out. These muffins are so good, you may want to make them and eat them without preparing a pudding. This has become a muffin recipe for my own kitchen. I discovered it at Canyon Villa B&B in Sedona, Arizona.

1/2	cup (1 stick) unsalted butter, softened
1 1/4	cups sugar
2	large eggs, room temperature
2	cups all-purpose flour
2	teaspoons baking powder
1/2	teaspoon salt
1/2	cup milk
2	cups fresh raspberries (or frozen berries thawed and drained)
4	teaspoons sugar

MAKES 12 TO 18 MUFFINS

*P*reheat the oven to 375°. Grease muffin tins. In a large bowl, cream the butter and 1 1/4 cups of sugar with an electric mixer until light and fluffy. Add the eggs, 1 at a time, beating well after each addition. In a small bowl, sift together the flour, baking powder, and salt. Add the dry ingredients to the butter mixture alternately with the milk. Fold in the berries. Divide the batter among the prepared muffin tins. Sprinkle the remaining 4 teaspoons of sugar over the batter. Bake for 30 minutes, or until a tester comes clean. Serve warm or at room temperature.

—GAIL'S KITCHEN

*A*lways carry teabags with you for those times when a restaurant offers you only one flavor. It happens to me often, but never at a B&B or country inn.

Directory

The Allen House
18 Allen Place
Scituate, MA 02066
(617) 545-8221

Rooms: 6

Tea-time: Afternoon
Christine Gilmour is a gourmet caterer and that enhances the splendid tea served daily at the inn for guests. The Allen House is surrounded by beach and salt marsh but is popular all year.

Amadeus House
15 Clifford Street
Lenox, MA 01240
(413) 637-4770

Rooms: 8

Tea-time: Afternoon for inn guests
It is everyone's dream: Live on a quiet street in a grand mansion and have only a five-minute walk to fine shops and restaurants. Make the dream come true in this exquisite inn, complete with rooms named Copeland, Brahms, and Schubert, reflecting the surrounding Berkshire region's wealth of great music and concerts.

Asa Ransom House
10529 Main Street
Clarence, NY 14031
(716) 759-2315

Rooms: 9

Tea-time: Thursdays from 2 p.m. to 4 p.m.—full afternoon tea, open to the public
After antiquing in Clarence, spend the night at the cozy Asa Ransom House. Enjoy country gourmet meals and select New York wines in a relaxing, historic environment.

Betsy's Bed & Breakfast
1428 Park Avenue
Baltimore, MD 21217
(410) 383-1274

Rooms: 3

Tea-time: Informal, daily, for guests only. Tea and sweets.
Bolton Hill is a refined, architecturally intriguing area of the old city of Baltimore, and Betsy's sits here—stately and inviting, complementing the area's history with period furnishings and traditions.

PICTURE FACING CHAPTER OPENER: A GARGOYLE AT RAVENWOOD CASTLE SUPPORTS THE THEORY THAT TEA CAN BE FUN.

Captain Swift Inn
72 Elm Street
Camden, ME 04843
(207) 236-8113

Rooms: 5

Tea-time: Informal, daily all afternoon in the parlor
The town of Camden, Maine is picture-postcard perfect with quaint shops and an old soda fountain drug store. The inn is a show-stopper, and the former home of the man who started windjammer cruising and established Maine's first passenger schooner fleet.

The Castle at Tarrytown
400 Benedict Avenue
Tarrytown, NY 10591
(914) 631-1980

Rooms: 7

Tea-time: Upon request
Awesome is the word to describe this special property. This is your chance to be treated like royalty—from the top-rated cuisine to the special guest rooms. Perched high on a hilltop overlooking the Hudson River, this authentic American castle is a treasure not to be missed.

The Davy Jackson Inn
85 Perry Avenue
Jackson Hole, Wyoming 83001
(307) 739-2294

Rooms: 11

Tea-time: Daily from 4 p.m., formal, sweets and savories, for guests; some reservations accepted for tea parties
This little Victorian in the midst of town serves a sumptuous afternoon tea in a small parlor. The food is delicious and served on lovely china. Whirlpools, fireplaces, and plush canopy beds make you want to stay in all day.

The Fearrington House
2000 Fearrington Village Center
Pittsboro, NC 27312
(919) 542-2121

Rooms: 15

Tea-time: 4 to 5 p.m. for inn guests
Beautiful gardens and rolling countryside encircle this classic inn. Built around a center courtyard, each guest room exudes its own distinctive character. The four-star restaurant features sophisticated regional cuisine.

Herb Haus Bed & Breakfast
P.O. Box 927
Fredericksburg, TX 78624
(210) 997-8615

Rooms: 2

Tea-time: 11:30 a.m. to 5 p.m. at The Tea Room
A little bit of the impressionist master painters and selections from children's garden tales fill the image of this B&B on fourteen acres of herbs, edible flowers, and country pleasures. The innkeepers own a small mail-order business with lotions and potions, and some good things to eat—all from their garden—plus a quarterly newsletter.

The Idaho Country Inn
134 Latigo Lane
Sun Valley, ID 83353
(208) 726-1019

Rooms: 10

Tea-time: Check-in time
Rave reviews from critics cite this B&B as outstanding. Each room has an individual lodge theme with warmth, charm, and plenty of exposed logs.

The Inn at 410
410 North Leroux Street
Flagstaff, AZ 86001
(520) 774-0088

Rooms: 9

Tea-time: All afternoon
They love tea so much here that they named one of the guest bedrooms The Tea Room, which has nothing to do with tea and everything to do with a king-sized bed, a whirlpool, and a fireplace. There is always something sweet cooking in the kitchen at this 1907, former wealthy banker/cattle rancher's place, built in craftsman style.

Inn at Georgian Place
800 Georgian Place Drive
Somerset, PA 15501
(814) 443-1043

Rooms: 11

Tea-time: Noon to 4 p.m., open to the public
A three-course English tea is served here in a most unusual B&B. The inn is elegant but unpretentious. A full breakfast is generous and only part of the wonderful pampering here.

The Inn at Maplewood Farm
447 Center Road
Hillsborough, NH 03244
(603) 464-4242

Rooms: 5

*Tea-time: Afternoons, informal, for
guests only*
Cheerful and enchanting, this small
farmhouse in the quiet countryside is truly
one of life's simple pleasures. Sip your tea
on the front porch and hear the jingle of the
authentic Swiss bells on a herd of neigh-
borly bovines. I'm not sure life gets any
better than this.

John Rutledge House Inn
116 Broad Street
Charleston, SC 29401
(803) 723-7999

Rooms: 21

Tea-time: Daily at arrival time
Linda Bishop is the innkeeper here and
she is dedicated to making sure that guests
receive the full antebellum experience. The
house was built in 1763 and John
Rutledge, a signer of the Declaration of
Independence, was its first owner.

The King's Cottage
1049 East King Street
Lancaster, PA 17602
(717) 397-1017

Rooms: 9

*Tea-time: 5 p.m., daily, informal, for
guests only, sweets and savories*
The name is a trusting one. They aim
to treat their guests like royalty here and
they do. Rooms are very tastefully decorated and very different. The converted car-
riage house is sumptuous.

Merry Sherwood Plantation Inn
8909 Worcester Highway
Berlin, MD 21811
(410) 641-2112

Rooms: 8

Tea-time: Check-in for guests
The serenity of days gone by is
omnipresent as this luxurious former plantation. Guests' rooms are spacious, comfortable, and decorated to the period, circa pre-
Civil War.

The *Pauline*
70 Elm Street
Camden, ME 04843
(207) 236-3520

Rooms: 6 cabins

Tea-time: On board while out at sea
Following a flourish of horns and whis-
tles, the 125-year-old schooner, The
Pauline, *glides gracefully from its slip for
an incredible adventure. Tea is served
from a silver tea set as the boat departs and
the journey gets off to a fine start.*

The Queen Anne Inn
420 West Washington Street
South Bend, ID 46601
234-5959

Rooms: 4

*Tea-time: Formal sit-down, sweet-
and-savory buffet, Thursdays 2–4 p.m. by
reservation for guests and open to the public.*

*The Queen Anne is an 1873 grand
Victorian townhouse with a friendly
innkeeper and delightful tables always set
for tea. Theme teas are held throughout the
year such as: Back-to-School Tea, Spring-
Hat Tea, and Tea-on-the-Porch.*

Ravenwood Castle
Route 1, Box 52-B
New Plymouth, OH 45654
(614) 596-2606

Rooms: 8

*Tea-time: 2 to 4 p.m., formal savories
and sweets in tea room for guests and the
public*

*Leave the modern world behind and
travel back about 800 years to the
Medieval countryside. Ravenwood guest
rooms are two-story turrets with modern
amenities. The castle was built as a replica
in 1995. It is a beauty and must be experi-
enced at least once in your lifetime. Tea
goodies are exceptional.*

Trillium
Route 2, Box 121
LaFarge, WI 54639
(608) 625-4492

Rooms: cottage

*Tea-time: At your own choice in the
cottage for guests only*

*A private cottage on the family farm
allows guests to view farm life. Livestock
are kept here along with fields and crops. A
full breakfast is served.*

Wild Swan Inn
525 Kings Highway
Lewes, DE 19958
(302) 645-8550

Rooms: 3

Tea-time: Check-in time
Delaware is not the first place you think about for a getaway. But it is a best-kept secret, especially in Lewes, a charming old maritime village. The inn is comfortable Victorian with spacious verandahs, perfect for taking time out with tea.

The Wildflower Inn
167 Palmer Avenue
Falmouth, MA 02540
(508) 548-9524

Rooms: 6

Tea-time: All day
A 1910 seaside home brimming with good spirit, good hearts, and great rooms. Cookies, pretzels, honey sticks for tea, and hot beverages are available right after breakfast. This is a must for any B&B-goer.

Index